PRAISE FOR *THE HEART OF A LEADER*

"*The Heart of a Leader: 52 Emotional Intelligence Insights to Advance Your Career* is a concise pocket-guide reference for navigating the career ecosystem. Kristin Harper has successfully created a toolkit to support leaders through the trenches of professional development." —**Ariana Martin**, DO, coauthor of *Her Story: Heartache, Happiness, and Hiccups Along the Way*

"If it comes from the heart, it sticks in the mind, and Harper has provided the glue: 52 high-EQ insights to help you ascend in a way that lets you keep your soul." —**Scott Mautz**, keynote speaker; author of *Make it Matter* and *Find the Fire*

"So you want to do better, and you want do good in this world. This is the book for you—and me. Harper's message and memoir tell us what it takes to succeed and how to be 'truly human.'" —**David Lawrence**, retired Miami Herald publisher; chair of The Children's Movement of Florida

The Heart of a Leader

The Heart of a Leader

52 Emotional Intelligence Insights to Advance Your Career

Kristin Harper

ROWMAN & LITTLEFIELD
Lanham · Boulder · New York · London

Published by Rowman & Littlefield
An imprint of The Rowman & Littlefield Publishing Group, Inc.
4501 Forbes Boulevard, Suite 200, Lanham, Maryland 20706
www.rowman.com

6 Tinworth Street, London SE11 5AL, United Kingdom

British Library Cataloguing in Publication Information Available

Library of Congress Cataloging-in-Publication Data

Names: Harper, Kristin, author.
Title: The heart of a leader : 52 emotional intelligence insights to advance your career /
    Kristin Harper.
Description: Lanham : Rowman & Littlefield, 2020. | Includes bibliographical
    references and index. | Summary: "Most employees are taught to work hard then wait
    to be recognized and rewarded. This has left millions of employees disappointed,
    dissatisfied, and stuck. Advancing your career requires not only technical competence
    (the "what") but also careful skills (the "how"). While some employees are lucky
    enough to have mentors to guide them along their career journey, even fewer have
    sponsors. This leaves a huge gap for millions of employees who aspire for more in
    their careers but lack a personal guide to help them navigate an uncertain and often
    treacherous job terrain. *The Heart of a Leader: 52 Emotional Intelligence Insights to
    Advance Your Career* uncovers insider secrets on leadership for go-getters who aren't
    satisfied with status quo careers. Authored by Kristin Harper, the book is based on
    over 20 years of firsthand experience climbing the proverbial corporate ladder. When
    Harper graduated from business school, she had the technical skills to succeed, but
    she wasn't equipped to navigate the politics, personalities, and changing priorities
    that accompany the work environment. Through a combination of hard work,
    sound guidance from mentors, and a commitment to continuous improvement, she
    was named vice president of a Fortune 15 company in her 30s. Strengthening her
    emotional intelligence (EI) was a critical enabler of her success. Now, she's sharing
    these insights with you"—Provided by publisher.
Identifiers: LCCN 2019057237 (print) | LCCN 2019057238 (ebook) | ISBN
    9781538132623 (cloth) | ISBN 9781538132630 (ebook)
Subjects: LCSH: Leadership—Psychological aspects. | Emotional intelligence. |
    Career development.
Classification: LCC BF637.L4 H367 2020 (print) | LCC BF637.L4 (ebook) |
    DDC 658.4/092—dc23
LC record available at https://lccn.loc.gov/2019057237
LC ebook record available at https://lccn.loc.gov/2019057238

To those who are committed to creating
better outcomes for their organizations
and experiencing a more satisfying career
that unleashes their potential

Contents

52 Emotional Intelligence Insights to Advance Your Career

1. Know thyself.
2. Bring your whole self to work, but be selective with what you share.
3. Dress for the job you want, not the job you have.
4. Instability reflects poorly on your capabilities.
5. Perception is reality.
6. Feedback is a gift that others don't have to give.
7. The common denominator might be you.
8. Quantify your impact, not your activities.
9. Say *yes* to the invite.
10. I'm ready for the next level. Now what?
11. Understand their mindset, motivations, and fears.
12. Strive to make your manager look good.
13. Some situations are above your paygrade.
14. Extend grace.
15. Forgive frequently.
16. Leadership is about learning as well as unlearning.
17. Call people by name.
18. Culture reigns supreme.
19. Clarity and accountability drive results.
20. Consider the trade-offs.
21. Be patient for growth.
22. Hire for character, not just competence.
23. Give your employees plenty of airtime.
24. Slow to hire, swift to fire.
25. Facts tell, but stories sell.

Foreword

$\mathscr{I}$ had the great pleasure to meet Kristin Harper several years ago at a Fortune 100 company where I served as an executive leadership coach. My coaching practice focuses on helping high-performing executives leverage emotional intelligence (EI) in order to develop their authentic personal brands, executive presence, and communication skills.

Like many high-achieving performers, Kristin had amassed an impressive track record of accomplishments throughout her career; however, she knew that drive alone was not a long-term strategy for sustainable success. She was ready to shift from "head to heart" in her practice of EI, recognizing it as an essential key to successfully and continuously rising to the next level.

Having coached or trained more than a thousand on-the-rise executives at some of the world's biggest companies, I know one thing holds true for all: at the next level of leadership they need an increased ability to influence and drive results through others. As they ascend in their organizations, they need more sophisticated and effective influencing and people skills.

Emotional intelligence is fundamental to developing the people skills needed to engage and influence others. It lies at the core of executive presence. Leaders who can identify and manage their own emotions *and* nimbly navigate the emotions of others tend to have stronger interpersonal relationships, greater executive presence, and more influence.

The challenge for most rising leaders is that EI can be an abstract concept. Emotions are complex and unwieldy and can seem out of place as an area of focus in a professional work setting. Practicing EI seems like it could take up a lot of valuable time that would be better spent just getting everyone to do their job.

The truth is, practicing EI is easy to do when it is translated into digestible, practical action steps. That is exactly what Kristin has done in *The Heart of a Leader: 52 Emotional Intelligence Insights to Advance Your Career*. She's adroitly put EI into a practical context by providing tips and practices aligned to workday situations that every leader faces at some point in their career.

Whether you are experiencing a bumpy relationship with your boss, needing to up-level your influencing skills, or having trouble navigating office politics, *The Heart of a Leader* provides you with bite-sized, easy-to-execute action steps. Some of the insights are intuitive, good old-fashioned common sense for professionals. Others are a fresh take on age-old career challenges. All of it is easy to access. Just grab, read, and go!

Wherever you are in your career, I highly recommend you add this book to your leadership toolbox. As Marshall Goldsmith famously wrote, "What got you here won't get you there." With *The Heart of a Leader*, Kristin has delivered a savvy playbook to get you there.

Rasheryl McCreary, PCC
CEO, TAO Leadership Development, Inc.

Acknowledgments

*F*irst and foremost, I thank God, who has given me the talent, passion, and will to realize my calling and purpose. Thank you for giving me the vision to write this book and to contribute to the world in a new, meaningful way. To Andre, my faithful husband, thank you for your enduring love, support, and wisdom. You've made so many sacrifices in support of my career growth and have been a steady hand through life's highs and lows. To our children, Celeste, Montgomery, and Prescott, thanks for being patient with Mommy when work obligations and travel took me away from you. Thank you to my mom and dad, Joan and Richard Tucker, for supporting every creative endeavor from baking cookies to writing books. Mom, the experiences you afforded me leading "Princess House crystal parties" at such a young age made me a confident communicator. This has been an invaluable asset in my life and career.

I owe who I am as a leader to some of my most influential role models in organizational leadership: Dr. Charles E. Booth, Dr. Frederick Humphries, Dr. Sybil Mobley, Pastor Damon Lynch, Jr., Matt Barresi, Diane Dietz, Alfredo Marrero, Jim Taylor, Roslyn Bolden, Diane Lorello, Rafa Garibay, Don Casey, Mike Kaufmann, George Barrett, Mike Duffy, Mike Buck, Valerie Pitteroff, Ramon Gregory, Kathryne Reeves, Nadine Thompson, Cynthia Butler-McIntyre, Pastor Jerry Revish, and Lady Danielle Revish. There are many other leaders who showed me how I did not wish to be. While they will remain nameless, their contributions have been just as valuable.

Thanks to my executive coach, Rasheryl McCreary, for helping to smooth out the rough edges and leading me on an amazing journey of self-discovery and refinement. You have been a blessing in my life, and

I am grateful to you for writing the foreword. Leonora, thank you for encouraging me to consider traditional publishing to share this message on a broader platform. Your mentorship, friendship, and generosity mean the world to me. To my friends and cheerleaders along this journey—Ariana and Kevin Martin, Beverlyn and Orvell Johns, Julius and Trishawnda Cabbagestalk, Sherry and Kevin Lloyd, Tramayne Whitney, James Booth, Nehal Patel, April Mills, Veronica Farris, Terrie Ragland, LaKesha Woodard, Natasha Austin, and so many others—thank you! Tashawna Otabil and Lawrence Brown, thank you for giving me the first opportunities to be a keynote speaker at your respective organizations.

Finally, to Leticia Gomez, my amazing literary agent, and my editor, Suzanne Staszak-Silva with Rowman & Littlefield Publishing, thanks for believing in me and this work. To Laraleigh Moffitt, thank you for editing my manuscript. You were invaluable. My sincere hope is that this book will transform the minds and heart of people around the world, both personally and professionally.

Introduction

Several years into my career, I had the great fortune of attending a week-long High Potential Leaders Program at Harvard Business School. In preparation for our daily classes, we read over a dozen case studies on actual businesses. In a matter of about twenty pages per case, we learned about the people involved, their titles, and their backgrounds. Cases included the business situation, the conflict, and the job to be done. There were accompanying graphs, charts, and visual aids to enhance the story. Yes, the story.

In class, the first series of discussions the professor initiated was not about the facts of the business; instead, it was about the characters. Who were they? What was the tension that needed to be resolved? How were they feeling?

"Feelings? What do feelings have to do with business?" I wondered.

The answer is: *everything*.

While I pride myself on being a logical leader who has consistently used analytics and insights to drive decisions, I had a light-bulb moment. Logic is not the only driver of people's words, actions, and behaviors; emotions matter too.

EMOTIONAL INTELLIGENCE

Intelligence and technical competence are important building blocks of performance. However, effective leadership requires both head and heart. The higher you go in your career, the more important personal and social competence becomes.

1

Peter Salovey and John D. Mayer first coined the term "emotional intelligence" in 1990, describing it as "a form of social intelligence that involves the ability to monitor one's own and others' feelings and emotions, to discriminate among them, and to use this information to guide one's thinking and action."[1]

The concept was made popular by author and journalist Daniel Goleman in 1995 and has since been the subject of numerous studies to validate the impact emotional intelligence has on job performance, mental health, and leadership skills. Goleman partnered with Richard Boyatzis at Case Western Reserve University to classify emotional intelligence into four domains and twelve competencies that distinguish leaders.[2]

Self-Awareness

- *Emotional Self-Awareness:* The ability to understand our own emotions and their effects on our performance.

Self-Management

- *Emotional Self-Control:* The ability to keep disruptive emotions and impulses in check and maintain our effectiveness under stressful or hostile conditions.
- *Achievement Orientation:* Striving to meet or exceed a standard of excellence; looking for ways to do things better, setting challenging goals, and taking calculated risks.
- *Positive Outlook:* The ability to see the positive in people, situations, and events; persistence in pursuing goals despite obstacles and setbacks.
- *Adaptability:* Flexibility in handling change, juggling multiple demands, and adapting our ideas or approaches.

Social Awareness

- *Empathy:* The ability to sense others' feelings and perspectives, take an active interest in their concerns, and pick up cues about what others feel and think.

- *Organizational Awareness:* The ability to read a group's emotional currents and power relationships and identify influencers, networks, and organizational dynamics.

Relationship Management

- *Influence:* The ability to have a positive impact on others, persuading or convincing others in order to gain their support.
- *Coach and Mentor:* The ability to foster the long-term learning or development of others by giving feedback, guidance, and support.
- *Conflict Management:* The ability to help others through emotional or tense situations by tactfully bringing disagreements into the open and finding solutions all can endorse.
- *Inspirational Leadership:* The ability to inspire and guide individuals and groups toward a meaningful vision of excellence; bringing out the best in others.
- *Teamwork:* The ability to work with others toward a shared goal; participating actively, sharing responsibility and rewards, and contributing to the capability of the team.

This book includes emotional intelligence insights based on nearly twenty years of personal leadership experience and climbing the proverbial corporate ladder at some of the world's leading Fortune 500 companies. While there's a story behind every pearl, the content is intentionally brief. We live in a fast-paced society with many competing priorities. If you're anything like me, you don't have time to waste.

Here's to your success!

• *1* •

Why Great Performance Isn't Enough

$\mathscr{I}$ve built my career managing some of the world's most iconic brands—Crest®, Oral-B®, and Hershey's KISSES®, to name a few. While there are many competitors to choose from in each of their respective categories, it's the power of these brands that make them stand out from the rest, demand a premium price versus generic competitors, and endear consumers across generations and geographies.

Brand management is the methodical process of establishing and maintaining the tangible and intangible attributes of a brand. Nearly every attribute of a well-managed brand is carefully researched and ultimately chosen based on what it delivers to the customers and how it makes them feel. This includes the four Ps—product, price, promotion, and placement. Brands are expressed across multiple senses through what we see, hear, smell, touch, and taste. Brands can also be crafted into an experience that evokes emotions to make you feel a certain way.

Like tangible goods and services, you, too, are a brand. Defining your unique brand fits squarely into emotional intelligence—self-awareness leads to self-management, which are two of the four domains of emotional intelligence. Before we get into the attributes of your unique brand, let's use Coca-Cola® as an example to establish some basic branding principles.

PRODUCT: COCA-COLA®

Coca-Cola originated in 1886 by pharmacist John Pemberton in Columbus, Georgia.[1] Well over a century later, its product portfolio remains strong and enduring.

There are four primary variants in the company's product portfolio—Coca-Cola®, Diet Coke®, Coca-Cola Zero Sugar®, and Coca-Cola Life®.[2] There are also several flavor variations, such as cherry, lemon, and vanilla. In addition to flavors, Coke has mastered the concept of usage occasions. There are different packages for various occasions, for example:

- Cans and bottles are for individual consumption.
- 2-liters are designed for sharing with a group, family, or friends during an event or to keep in a refrigerator and consume over time.
- 1-liters are smaller footprint bottles for limited consumption by an individual or a smaller group of people.
- Miniature cans offer portion control for individual consumption.

Price

The price strategy has an impact on the "brand equity," which is what the brand stands for in the hearts and minds of its customers or consumers. Pricing is determined by several factors, including

- The unique attributes of the product or service.
- Its ability to meet an unmet need among a specific target audience.
- The consumers' ability to pay.
- Market conditions.
- Competitive landscape.
- The cost of manufacturing and raw materials.
- Desired profit margins.

In general, there are three basic types of pricing strategies:

1. Premium Pricing—these brands are priced above most competitors. They can command a premium price due to their brand image, features, benefits, and/or limited availability due to the principle of supply and demand. Pricing at a premium could mean that fewer customers purchase the brand; however, the profit margins are higher, and it may lead to higher overall profit for the brand. Premium pricing and profit margins allow brands to create a more exclusive customer experience and offer steeper promotional discounts to persuade customers to purchase their products or services.
2. Market Pricing—these brands are priced in line with competitors. Generally, there are multiple competitors who each have a sizable customer base. Often, there are frequent promotions to persuade customers to purchase their brand and to steal market share from competitors. Innovation tends to be more frequent because it helps bring news to the brand and a competitive category.
3. Value Pricing—the goal for these brands is to gain as much unit volume and market share as possible through a low-price strategy. Low prices often mean that the product quality is subpar compared to more expensive brands. They are more easily substituted, which erodes their brand equity and leads to being perceived as a commodity. Value-priced brands lack the margins to invest in research and development and are often fast followers or laggards of more innovative market- or premium-priced brands.

Coca-Cola utilizes market pricing strategy. According to Amazon, a 12-ct. of 12 oz. Coca-Cola cans costs $4.99, compared to $5.13 for 12 cans of Pepsi®. Pricing is virtually equivalent.

Promotion

Brand managers and their advertising agency partners develop a carefully crafted image of brands in the hearts and minds of the target audience. This is done by increasing brand awareness with its advertisements, website, social media, and the careful selection of people and images associated with the brand. Promotion also includes discounting the price, offering freebies, and other "buy X, get Y" offers periodically to drive loyalty, impulse purchases, and switching from competitive brands.

Coca-Cola has delivered some of the world's most iconic promotions. Considered to be "the world's most famous ad," Coca-Cola launched a television ad entitled "I'd Like to Buy the World a Coke" in 1971.[3] Bill Backer, the creative who envisioned the advertisement, wrote the scene after an overnight travel delay that left him and other tourists frustrated and angry. The next morning, these once disgruntled travelers were more happy and joyful as they communed around sips of Coca-Cola. He wrote:

> In that moment [I] saw a bottle of Coke in a whole new light. . . .
> [I] began to see a bottle of Coca-Cola as more than a drink that re-
> freshed a hundred million people a day in almost every corner of the
> globe. So [I] began to see the familiar words, "Let's have a Coke," as
> more than an invitation to pause for refreshment. They were actually
> a subtle way of saying, "Let's keep each other company for a little
> while." And [I] knew they were being said all over the world as [I]
> sat there in Ireland. So that was the basic idea: to see Coke not as it
> was originally designed to be—a liquid refresher—but as a tiny bit
> of commonality between all peoples, a universally liked formula that
> would help to keep them company for a few minutes.[4]

The song first aired on the radio in February 1971, gaining nearly immediate popularity. Listeners repeatedly requested the song, and it peaked at number 7 on the *Billboard* Hot 100, according to *Billboard*.[5] Airing in the United States in the midst of the Vietnam War that began in 1955, the song brought a message of peace and hope to a dark time in America. Soon thereafter, the famous jingle was the backdrop of a television ad with five hundred people of all shapes, colors, and ethnicities standing on a hilltop in Manziana, Italy. Coca-Cola received over a hundred thousand letters about the advertisement.

Even today, Coke is about so much more than a carbonated soft drink. Its emotional benefits are about happiness, family, and community, and this serves as the centerpiece of advertising and promotions. According to their corporate website, Coca-Cola, recognized as the world's most valuable brand, is often associated with happiness. In fact, Coca-Cola means "Delicious Happiness" in Mandarin.[6]

Placement

I've been blessed to travel to five continents, and Coca-Cola is ubiquitous in retailers, vending machines, and restaurants around the world. According to its website, the Coca-Cola Company is the world's largest beverage company, with an operational reach spanning over two hundred countries worldwide. While there are twenty-one billion-dollar brands within the company's portfolio, the red and white Coca-Cola logo of its namesake parent brand is recognized by 94 percent of the world's population.[7] That's one more reason Coke is best in class when it comes to brands.

In addition to the four Ps of marketing, a brand engages people's emotions by influencing their senses (see table 1.1).

Table 1.1. Sense and Experience of Marketing

Sense	Experience
Sight	Product packaging
	• The iconic glass Coke bottle is shaped unlike that of any competitor. I'd bet that if the words were removed from the bottle or you closed your eyes and felt its shape, you would be able to recognize the brand. This is one reason its iconic bottle is patented and still recognizable more than a hundred years later.
	Font
	• The brand uses a distinguishing cursive font.
	Color palette
	• Red and white are the signature colors, and there are specific pantone colors their teams must abide by for consistency. A crimson red or creamy white color, for example, would be "off equity" and inappropriate for use with the Coca-Cola brand.
	• As the brand has introduced new product innovation and targeted different audiences, more colors have been added to the palette. For example, black is the primary color for Coke Zero, a product launched in 2005 originally targeted toward men.[1] Coke Life is a more recent product launch that utilizes a green color to reinforce the benefit of being a lower-calorie cola made with a blend of cane sugar and stevia leaf extract, which is perceived to be a more natural option.
	• When you open a can of Coke, you can see small carbonated bubbles, reinforcing its benefit of refreshment. Even the bubbles play a role in its brand.

(continued)

Table 1.1. (continued)

Sense	Experience
Hearing	Coca-Cola name • Its trademark name clearly indicates the product category of cola. • Like a beloved family member or friend, Coca-Cola also has a nickname that is endearing to many people—Coke. • Since Coca-Cola has been a category leader across many decades, "Coke" has become synonymous with the category. For example, some people call other brands and even soda flavors Coke. In these instances, it's important for a brand to drive its points of difference to avoid becoming generic and losing its brand value. • When you open a can of Coke, you can also hear the sound of refreshment as carbon dioxide is released to form bubbles. This sound is often included in its advertising and pays off with the idea of refreshment.
Smell and Taste	Distinctive formula • Coca-Cola has a proprietary "secret formula" originally used by pharmacist John Pemberton when he first mixed the drink in 1886 in Columbus, Georgia. Its combination of sugar, spices, and flavors creates a fragrant aroma of cinnamon, lime, lemon, orange, coriander, vanilla, and nutmeg.[2] Many have tried unsuccessfully to duplicate the secret recipe, and it will always remain in the company's best interest to fiercely guard its proprietary formula and manufacturing process.
Touch	Carbonated bubbles • The carbon dioxide in a fresh can or glass of Coca-Cola creates a tangy, crisp explosion of carbonated bubbles that seem to leap off the tongue. When the product loses its carbonation, the brand experience is eroded.

1. Olivia Chang, "Coca-Cola Is Replacing Coke Zero with a New Drink," CNN Money, July 26, 2017, https://money.cnn.com/2017/07/26/news/companies/coke-zero/index.html.

2. "Coca-Cola," Fragrantica, https://www.fragrantica.com/notes/Coca-Cola-362.html, last modified 2019.

Hopefully you now have a better understanding of attributes that form a powerful, enduring brand. Now, let's apply these principles to your personal brand so that you can advance your career.

PRODUCT: YOU

What is your personal value proposition? That is, a positioning statement that explains what benefit you provide for whom and how you do it uniquely well?[8] What do you offer that fulfills an unmet need for your target audience? What benefits and value do you provide that differentiates you from "competition"?

For example:

- Financial Advisor: I provide a path to financial freedom in seven years or less.
- HR Professional: I cultivate talent to address business solutions.
- Researcher/R&D: I match unmet needs with inventive solutions.
- Communication Professional: I make the complex simple.
- Marketer: I transform insights into brand-building results.

Crafting these short, pithy statements may seem like an easy task, but it requires deep reflection and several rounds of edits to capture the essence of a powerful, provocative, and enduring brand. Let's break down the process, which I refer to as a Personal Brand Audit, shown in figure 1.1.

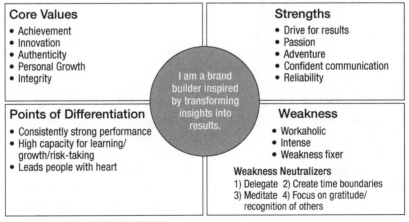

Figure 1.1. Personal Brand Audit

A Personal Brand Audit

Step 1: Establish Your Core Values
What are your fundamental beliefs? These are often shaped in childhood and through life experience. For example:

- I began a business at the tender age of fourteen—Krissy's Cookies 'n' Stuff. I needed money to buy Christmas gifts for my family and friends, so I turned to a skill my mother taught me—baking. On Saturday nights, I would stay up until the wee hours of the morning baking cookies, cakes, and pies for church members. That Christmas, I earned $100 profit, a healthy amount of money for an eighth-grade student. That experience shaped the core values of hard work, achievement, and reward.
- I married my college sweetheart in a ceremony with over three hundred guests, but after nine short months of marriage, we separated and soon divorced. It was a painful experience, to say the least. However, I took the next two years to invest in myself and become a better person from the inside out. He did the same. Miraculously, three years after we separated, my husband and I remarried and have been together ever since. Because of this experience, I believe in forgiveness and second chances for those who are willing to put in the work for a better future.

Table 1.2 includes a list of core values to consider.

Step 2: Define Your Strengths and Weaknesses
What is your primary skill set? What can you do better than most people? What are the areas that don't come naturally to you or could hold you back? I'm a huge advocate for two tools that drive self-awareness: (1) 360 feedback, and (2) the CliftonStrengths® assessment, formerly known as StrengthsFinder®.

360 feedback provides a snapshot of how you're viewed by others compared to how you view yourself. It's an anonymous opportunity for others to assess key characteristics on what you deliver and how you do it.

360 assessments come in many forms. There are companies who offer the service with sophisticated analysis, and there are many free online survey tools that provide anonymity. In its most simple form, you can ask others for their overall impressions of you—strengths, op-

Table 1.2. Core Values

Above and
Beyond
Acceptance
Accessibility
Accomplishment
Accountability
Accuracy
Accurate
Achievement
Activity
Adaptability
Adventure
Adventurous
Affection
Affective
Aggressive
Agility
Aggressiveness
Alert
Alertness
Altruism
Ambition
Amusement
Anti-Bureaucratic
Anticipate
Anticipation
Anti-Corporate
Appreciation
Approachability
Approachable
Assertive
Assertiveness
Attention to
Detail
Attentive
Attentiveness
Availability
Available
Awareness
Balance
Beauty
Being the Best
Belonging
Best

Best People
Bold
Boldness
Bravery
Brilliance
Brilliant
Calm
Calmness
Candor
Capability
Capable
Careful
Carefulness
Caring
Certainty
Challenge
Change
Character
Charity
Cheerful
Citizenship
Clean
Cleanliness
Clear
Clear-Minded
Clever
Clients
Collaboration
Comfort
Commitment
Common Sense
Communication
Community
Compassion
Competence
Competency
Competition
Competitive
Completion
Composure
Comprehensive
Concentration
Concern for
Others

Confidence
Confidential
Confidentiality
Conformity
Connection
Consciousness
Consistency
Content
Contentment
Continuity
Continuous
Improvement
Contribution
Control
Conviction
Cooperation
Coordination
Cordiality
Correct
Courage
Courtesy
Craftiness
Craftsmanship
Creation
Creative
Creativity
Credibility
Cunning
Curiosity
Customer Focus
Customer
Satisfaction
Customer Service
Customers
Daring
Decency
Decisive
Decisiveness
Dedication
Delight
Democratic
Dependability
Depth
Determination

Determined
Development
Devotion
Devout
Different
Differentiation
Dignity
Diligence
Direct
Directness
Discipline
Discovery
Discretion
Diversity
Dominance
Down-to-Earth
Dreaming
Drive
Duty
Eagerness
Ease of Use
Economy
Education
Effective
Effectiveness
Efficiency
Efficient
Elegance
Empathy
Employees
Empower
Empowering
Encouragement
Endurance
Energy
Engagement
Enjoyment
Entertainment
Enthusiasm
Entrepreneurship
Environment
Equality
Equitable
Ethical

(*continued*)

Table 1.2. (continued)

Exceed	Frugality	Inquisitive	Meritocracy
Expectations	Fun	Insight	Meticulous
Excellence	Generosity	Insightful	Mindful
Excitement	Genius	Inspiration	Moderation
Exciting	Giving	Integrity	Modesty
Exhilarating	Global	Intelligence	Motivation
Exuberance	Goodness	Intensity	Mystery
Experience	Goodwill	International	Neatness
Expertise	Gratitude	Intuition	Nerve
Exploration	Great	Intuitive	No Bureaucracy
Explore	Greatness	Invention	Obedience
Expressive	Growth	Investing	Open
Extrovert	Guidance	Investment	Open-Minded
Fairness	Happiness	Inviting	Openness
Faith	Hard Work	Irreverence	Optimism
Faithfulness	Harmony	Irreverent	Order
Family	Health	Joy	Organization
Family	Heart	Justice	Original
Atmosphere	Helpful	Kindness	Originality
Famous	Heroism	Knowledge	Outrageous
Fashion	History	Leadership	Partnership
Fast	Holiness	Learning	Passion
Fearless	Honesty	Legal	Patience
Ferocious	Honor	Level-Headed	Patient-Centered
Fidelity	Hope	Liberty	Patient-Focused
Fierce	Hopeful	Listening	Patients
Firm	Hospitality	Lively	Patient
Fitness	Humble	Local	Satisfaction
Flair	Humility	Logic	Patriotism
Flexibility	Humor	Longevity	Peace
Flexible	Hygiene	Love	People
Fluency	Imagination	Loyalty	Perception
Focus	Impact	Mastery	Perceptive
Focus on Future	Impartial	Maturity	Perfection
Foresight	Impious	Maximizing	Performance
Formal	Improvement	Maximum	Perseverance
Fortitude	Independence	Utilization	Persistence
Freedom	Individuality	Meaning	Personal
Fresh	Industry	Meekness	Development
Fresh Ideas	Informal	Mellow	Personal Growth
Friendly	Innovation	Members	Persuasive
Friendship	Innovative	Merit	Philanthropy

Play	Reflection	Serenity	Tolerance
Playfulness	Relationships	Serious	Tough
Pleasantness	Relaxation	Service	Toughness
Poise	Reliability	Shared Prosperity	Traditional
Polish	Reliable	Sharing	Training
Popularity	Resilience	Shrewd	Tranquility
Positive	Resolute	Significance	Transparency
Potency	Resolution	Silence	Trust
Potential	Resolve	Silliness	Trustworthy
Power	Resourceful	Simplicity	Truth
Powerful	Resourcefulness	Sincerity	Understanding
Practical	Respect	Skill	Unflappable
Pragmatic	Respect for	Skillfulness	Unique
Precise	Others	Smart	Uniqueness
Precision	Respect for the	Solitude	Unity
Prepared	Individual	Speed	Universal
Preservation	Responsibility	Spirit	Useful
Pride	Responsiveness	Spirituality	Utility
Privacy	Rest	Spontaneous	Valor
Proactive	Restraint	Stability	Value
Proactively	Results	Standardization	Value Creation
Productivity	Results-Oriented	Status	Variety
Profane	Reverence	Stealth	Victorious
Professionalism	Rigor	Stewardship	Victory
Profitability	Risk	Strength	Vigor
Profits	Risk-Taking	Structure	Virtue
Progress	Rule of Law	Succeed	Vision
Prosperity	Sacrifice	Success	Vital
Prudence	Safety	Support	Vitality
Punctuality	Sanitary	Surprise	Warmth
Purity	Satisfaction	Sustainability	Watchful
Pursue	Security	Sympathy	Watchfulness
Pursuit	Self-Awareness	Synergy	Wealth
Quality	Self-Motivation	Systemization	Welcoming
Quality of Work	Self-	Talent	Willfulness
Rational	Responsibility	Teamwork	Winning
Real	Self-Control	Temperance	Wisdom
Realistic	Self-Directed	Thankful	Wonder
Reason	Selfless	Thorough	Worldwide
Recognition	Self-Reliance	Thoughtful	Work/Life
Recreation	Sense of Humor	Timeliness	Balance
Refined	Sensitivity	Timely	

"Core Values Examples," Threads Culture, accessed November 1, 2018, https://www.threadsculture.com/core-values-examples/.

portunities, and what impact your actions have on them, intentional or otherwise. It's a best practice to get this information in writing, as it enables the feedback provider to offer thoughtful, anonymous feedback. 360s also give the receiver an opportunity to fully digest and reflect on the feedback now and in the future.

Consider asking for feedback from employees, your manager, peers, family, friends, relatives, clients, mentors, and fellow members of boards, clubs, and organizations. Although your primary goal is to advance your career, it's important to ask for feedback outside of the workplace. Every situation includes a different set of dynamics, and we reveal different aspects of who we are depending on that context. For example, at work the stakes are high, so you may be more measured with your words. In a club or organization, where your income and livelihood aren't at risk, you may be more liberal in sharing your perspective and opinions. You're the same person, just in a different context. Therefore, the impressions others have of you could differ, and the diverse feedback is valuable.

In addition to a series of consistent questions asked of every respondent, 360 assessments provide an opportunity for open-ended feedback, also known as verbatims. Picture yourself as an adorable, loving cat. If you looked in the mirror, what would you expect to see? An adorable, loving cat highlighting all your strengths and amazing qualities. A 360 feedback report can affirm the image we have of ourselves, but sometimes the results are surprising. What others might see is a ferocious lion instead.

Drama aside, 360 assessments can be humbling. Of course, we believe we're amazing (and we are), but sometimes there are blind spots we're not aware of that are as plain as day to others. These blind spots can be difficult to articulate, especially unprompted in the course of daily work or even performance reviews. These often come to light in a 360 assessment.

"Perception is reality." This was the first lesson I learned on day one of attending the School of Business and Industry at Florida A&M University. Even if I don't agree or think it's true, if it's how I'm perceived by someone else, it is true to them. Therefore, it's in my best interest to take heed of the feedback, however easy or difficult it may be. 360 assessments help to crystalize our strengths and clarify our opportunities for growth.

I was once assigned to a project with an aggressive launch date. I was asked to launch dozens of new products in eighteen months, which is a process that typically takes two to three years for a handful of products. The composition of my direct team included one experienced marketer and three employees who were new to marketing and product management. Given the aggressive target, I should have balanced the team with more experienced talent. I get great joy from developing others, but the time pressure of the initiative proved to be a challenge with a willing, capable, yet inexperienced team.

The project required detailed project planning, extensive cross-functional engagement, and accountability, as well as long days and nights. I am proud to report that our small but mighty team introduced over 160 product SKUs in sixteen months. The "what" was an impressive accomplishment. However, the "how" was a different story. The team's feedback came through loud and clear on a 360 assessment. What I perceived as "on-the-job coaching to build their capability while delivering an aggressive goal" showed up to my direct reports as micromanaging.

In hindsight, I had transitioned from another industry and organization where fifty to sixty hour work weeks were the norm. I was used to working tirelessly to accomplish mutual goals and expected that my team would exhibit this same work ethic. I know that Achiever is my number one talent on the CliftonStrengths assessment, which we will discuss in the next section. When I'm at my best, my Achiever side shows up as being a tireless go-getter, leading by example, and having a strong work ethic. However, when the Achiever strength is overutilized, I can have a hard time saying no, which leads to being overcommitted, unbalanced, sleep-deprived, and laser focused on the task at hand.

I was still learning my new company and neglected to realize the organizational impact my actions and unspoken expectations were having on my team. They were burned-out. They felt like I didn't trust them. That was partially true, since it's difficult to extend unilateral trust to someone doing a task for the first time, no matter how capable and eager they are to learn. However, I was so focused on achieving the task that I powered through without demonstrating organizational awareness or empathy for others.

The 360 assessment was beneficial for several reasons: it helped affirm my strengths, pointed out blind spots in my personal approach, and persuaded me to more deeply understand the organizational culture.

Long hours may have been the norm in other companies, but it was an anomaly in that company's culture.

360 feedback can also unearth strengths you may not realize you have. In a recent 360 assessment, seven leadership competencies rose to the top as consistent themes. The most dominant theme was visioning—developing and executing strategy and thinking about the big picture. Prior to receiving this feedback, I would have identified this as an attribute but not a towering strength. I now see myself the way others see me: as a visionary leader.

While 360 assessments calibrate feedback from several people, CliftonStrengths, which I will also refer to as Strengths, helps individuals discover what they naturally do best, learn how to develop their greatest talents, improve self-awareness, explain who they are to others, and improve their performance.[9] An alternative to the typical psychological approach to diagnose what's "wrong" with a person, the CliftonStrengths test uses positive psychology by focusing on what's "right" and identifying their strengths, from most dominant to least.

The original StrengthsFinder test, developed by the Gallup organization, was first publicized in 2001 with the self-help book *Now, Discover Your Strengths* by Marcus Buckingham and Donald Clifton, who was the chairman of Gallup. I think of Strengths as a personality DNA, that is, the characteristics that feel natural to you and are almost effortless. According to Gallup, "a strength is the ability to consistently provide near-perfect performance in a specific activity. Talents are naturally recurring patterns of thought, feeling, or behavior that can be productively applied. Talents, knowledge, and skills—along with the time spent practicing, developing your skills, and building your knowledge base—combine to create your strengths."[10]

There are thirty-four strengths, or themes, that are universal among people around the world. In the customized report, these themes are ranked high to low based on the dominance of your talents. The more dominant your talents are within a theme, the higher that theme will appear in rank order. The chances of having the exact same Top 5 Talent Themes in the exact order as someone else is 1 in 33.39 million. The chances of having the same Top 5 Talent Themes as someone else, but in a different order, is approximately 1 in 340,000.[11] Therefore, Strengths really illustrates how unique you truly are. The insights from this short assessment can be profound in defining your strengths, weaknesses, and what makes you uniquely you. This assessment can be found in the book *StrengthsFinder 2.0* by Tom Rath.

The four domains and thirty-four strengths[12] are as follows.

Executing Strengths The nine Executing strengths relate to taking action, getting things done, implementing ideas, and making things happen. People with strengths in the Executing domain can take an idea and make it a reality.

- Achiever
- Arranger
- Belief
- Consistency
- Deliberative
- Discipline
- Focus
- Responsibility
- Restorative

Influencing Strengths The eight Influencing strengths relate to communication, persuasion, the ability to influence others, and sales. People with strengths in the Influencing domain can take an idea, speak up, and sell the idea to others.

- Activator
- Command
- Communication
- Competition
- Maximizer
- Self-Assurance
- Significance
- Woo

Relationship Building Strengths The nine Relationship Building strengths relate to people, relationships, individuals and teams, and human connectedness. People with strengths in the Relationship Building domain can bring people together and keep them together, creating a team that is greater than the sum of its parts.

- Adaptability
- Connectedness
- Developer
- Empathy
- Harmony
- Includer
- Individualization
- Positivity
- Relator

Strategic Thinking Strengths   The eight Strategic Thinking strengths relate to absorbing information, strategizing, coming up with plans, understanding situations, and predicting outcomes. People with strengths in the Strategic Thinking domain can plan for the future and focus on what "could be," always absorbing and analyzing information in order to make better decisions.

- Analytical
- Context
- Futuristic
- Ideation
- Input
- Intellection
- Learner
- Strategic

Step 3: Match Your Strengths to the Target Position or Career Experience
When there is alignment between your natural strengths and the requirements to be successful in a given role, you can experience momentum. Connect the dots for your manager and other influencers by consistently demonstrating your competence with multiple "proof points" of your achievements. Document these tangible accomplishments, then communicate the "reasons to believe" when you express your interest in and alignment to your target role. Don't leave this up to chance or wait for someone else to tap you on the shoulder. Advancing your career is not an exercise in humility; it requires intention, strategic action, and proactive communication.

Step 4: Neutralize Your Weaknesses

Leaders are deeply human and deeply imperfect. Identify, then close the gaps in skill set, character, or experience necessary to advance your career. If the weakness is a gap in skill set or experience, neutralize your weaknesses by learning "just enough to be dangerous" while acknowledging that you are not, and will not be, an expert. You can also select talented team members who compensate for your shortcomings or mentor you while you build greater competence and comfort.

When we have character flaws that can sabotage our potential, self-awareness, journaling, meditating, and working with a coach or accountability partner are proven strategies that can neutralize your weaknesses. Taking quiet time for reflection is also powerful for self-awareness.

When we were growing up, you may have heard the phrase, "You can do anything you put your mind to." While that sounds uplifting, the truth is that there are some skills that we will never master, no matter how hard we work at them. The premise of CliftonStrengths is about identifying your natural talents, not fixing your weaknesses. Capitalize on what comes naturally to you, and minimize anything that could derail you from achieving your potential.

Step 5: Clarify Your Points of Differentiation

Remember the concept of a brand (Coca-Cola versus a generic cola)? We all have a competitive set. While we don't have to be cutthroat, passive-aggressive, or overly competitive, it is important to understand who, or what, could be a close substitute for what you deliver. Who has similar knowledge, skills, and abilities? Who could fulfill your roles and responsibilities as well as or better than you? Who, or what else, can get the job done for the end customer? I say who or what because offshore talent, artificial intelligence, and other technological advances are disrupting the norms every single day and will inevitably result in job elimination that saves companies money. The pace of change and the competitive nature of every industry is accelerating.

Now that you've identified your competitive set, identify what benefits they deliver, what makes them unique, and how they position themselves with the target audience. Do the same for yourself, with a focus on identifying benefits that are

- Desirable—it's what the customer or organization wants;
- Distinctive—it's a differentiated versus competitive set; and

- Deliverable—they're not just an aspiration because you can actually "deliver the goods" and produce the results.

Step 6: Define Your Brand Character
What are the personality attributes of your brand? If we were doing this exercise for a brand like Coca-Cola, we would think about which human characteristics would be true for the brand. When demonstrated over time, brand character shapes behaviors that form your brand equity, which is what you stand for in the hearts and minds of your target audience.

When I lead brand positioning workshops, an easy introduction to this concept is to ask: "If you were a car, what type of car would you be and why?" At its core, an automobile is a vehicle that transports someone from one place to another. However, brand managers have shaped otherwise functional automobiles into distinct brands that establish identity and evoke emotion. It's not simply an aspirational exercise. These attributes must be "paid off" with proof points, also known as "reasons to believe."

For example, BMW is known as the "ultimate driving machine." Let's look at the desirable, distinct functional and emotional brand characteristics and how BMW delivers against these promises to their customers.

Brand Characteristic:	High performance
Reason to Believe:	German engineering
Brand Characteristic:	Luxury
Reasons to Believe:	Aspirational personas of drivers, attention to even nuanced details
Brand Characteristic:	Precise and powerful
Reason to Believe:	Hugs the sharpest curves with grace and speed

Other automobile and motor vehicle brands and personalities include

- Volvo—safe
- Subaru—adventurous
- Toyota—reliable
- Harley Davidson—irreverent

In addition to self-reflection, the results of your 360 assessment can provide insight into your brand character attributes. The following tables provide lists of personality characteristics that can serve as thought starters for your exploration. The attributes in table 1.3 are considered positive. Table 1.4 lists attributes that are generally opportunities or weaknesses.

Table 1.3. Positive Personality Characteristics

active	curious	independent	persistent
adaptable	daring	individualistic	planful
adventurous	deliberate	industrious	pleasant
affected	dependable	informal	poised
affectionate	dependent	ingenious	polished
alert	determined	initiative	practical
ambitious	dignified	insightful	praising
appreciative	direct	intelligent	precise
artistic	discreet	interesting	progressive
assertive	dispassionate	inventive	quick
attractive	dreamy	jolly	quiet
autocratic	easy-going	kind	rational
balanced	efficient	leisurely	realistic
calm	emotional	logical	reasonable
capable	energetic	loud	reflective
careless	enterprising	loyal	relaxed
caring	enthusiastic	mannerly	reliable
cautious	excitable	mature	reserved
changeable	fair-minded	meek	resourceful
charming	foresighted	methodical	responsible
cheerful	forgiving	mild	retiring
civilized	formal	moderate	robust
clear-thinking	frank	modern	self-assured
clever	friendly	modest	self-confident
commonplace	fun	natural	self-controlled
competent	fun-loving	obliging	self-denying
confident	generous	opinionated	sensitive
conscientious	gentle	opportunistic	sentimental
conservative	good-natured	optimistic	serious
considerate	healthy	organized	sharp-witted
contemporary	helpful	original	shy
contented	high-strung	outgoing	silent
conventional	honest	outspoken	simple
cool	humorous	patient	sincere
cooperative	idealistic	peaceable	sociable
courageous	imaginative	persevering	soft

(continued)

Table 1.3. (*continued*)

softhearted	strong	tolerant	versatile
sophisticated	submissive	touchy	vigorous
spendthrift	suggestible	trusting	warm
spontaneous	sympathetic	unaffected	wary
spunky	tactful	unassuming	wholesome
stable	talkative	unconventional	wise
steady	thorough	understanding	witty
stern	thoughtful	unemotional	zany
stingy	thrifty	uninhibited	
straightforward	timid	unselfish	

Table 1.4. Negative Personality Characteristics

abrasive	distractible	irresponsible	selfish
absentminded	distrustful	irritable	severe
aggressive	dominant	lazy	shallow
aloof	dull	mischievous	shiftless
anxious	egotistical	moody	show-off
apathetic	evasive	nagging	shrewd
argumentative	fault-finding	nervous	slow
arrogant	fearful	noisy	sly
awkward	fickle	obnoxious	smug
bitter	foolish	painstaking	snobbish
blustery	forceful	peculiar	spineless
boastful	forgetful	pessimistic	stubborn
bossy	frivolous	prejudiced	sulky
careless	fussy	preoccupied	suspicious
coarse	gloomy	prickly	temperamental
cold	greedy	prudish	tense
complaining	hardheaded	quarrelsome	thankless
complicated	hard-hearted	quitting	tough
conceited	hasty	rattlebrained	unambitious
confused	headstrong	rebellious	unfriendly
coward	hostile	reckless	unkind
cruel	hurried	resentful	unrealistic
cynical	immature	restless	unscrupulous
deceitful	impatient	rigid	unstable
defensive	impulsive	rude	vindictive
demanding	indifferent	sarcastic	weak
despondent	infantile	self-centered	withdrawn
disorderly	inhibited	self-pitying	worrying
disorganized	intolerant	self-punishing	
dissatisfied	intrusive	self-seeking	

Completing this fundamental background is critical to enhance self-awareness and establish brand "you." Now it's time to complete your "I am . . ." statement, which is the first P in your four Ps exercise—product, or unique value proposition. Once you complete the "I am . . ." statement, your Personal Brand Audit will be complete.

The remaining Ps—pricing, promotion, and placement—are part of your personal positioning. See table 1.5. While a bit more difficult to translate from a tangible product to a personal brand, the senses represent the brand experience other people will have with you in person and online, as shown in table 1.6.

Table 1.5. Product, Pricing, Promotion, and Placement

Attribute	Definition	Example
Product	What do you offer? What value do you bring?	I transform insights into brand building results.
Pricing	Based on how you are positioned, can you command a premium price, are you in line with the market, or are you value-priced?	I am positioned to command a premium price based on a track record of tangible results, business and organizational cross-industry experience, and brand reputation.
Promotion	How do you establish your brand reputation and drive awareness?	My performance reviews, mentoring/ networking conversations, and professional activities provide exposure and reinforce my value as a brand builder who transforms insights into results.
Placement	In which channels do you gain exposure and visibility with others? (i.e., companies, teams, industries, organizations, communities, traditional media, social media, etc.)	• I use LinkedIn to nurture my professional brand reputation online. • I am a member of industry organizations and attend relevant conferences to sharpen my skills and network with other practitioners. • I contribute functional expertise as a board member for a nonprofit organization. • I serve as a company recruiter and motivational speaker with college students.

Table 1.6.   Senses and Brand Experience

Sense	Experience
Sight	• Do you dress appropriately for your organizational culture? • Does your style reinforce your desired brand image and career aspiration, even on "business casual" days? • Are your hair, nails, and makeup well-groomed? • Is your smile sincere? • Do your interactions with others support your desired brand character?
Hearing	• Is your tone of voice consistent with your brand character? • Do you listen well to others? • Do you invite other people to make contributions to the conversation? • Do you accept feedback without being defensive?
Smell, Taste, and Touch	• How do people feel when they're with you? • Are you sensitive to the needs and feelings of others? • Do you recognize social cues and respond appropriately?

Once you complete this important foundational work, you are ready to complete your Personal Brand Pyramid. What's the difference between these two tools? Think of the Personal Brand Audit as a raw, unfiltered inventory of who you are—the good, the bad, and the ugly. Typically, this is more static. Oftentimes, our strengths and opportunities have been consistent over time. We just learn to navigate by dialing up or down our natural tendencies.

Personal Brand Pyramid

The Personal Brand Pyramid is a more refined, polished representation of how you show up to others. This is more flexible and can change over time with intention and focus. While some of the content can be the same between the Personal Brand Audit and Personal Brand Pyramid, it is perfectly acceptable to make modifications. After all, the audiences for each tool are different—you and the world.

Step 1: Define Your Target Role or Experience

Think about your career aspirations. What is your target role or experience? We often think about a title; however, with the rapid pace of change, new positions are being created and existing positions are

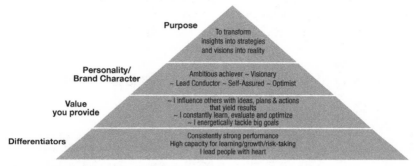

Target Role/Experience: C-suite/Senior Leadership/General Manager

Target Audience: Manager, mentors, sponsor, current C-suite, cross-functional peers

Purpose — To transform insights into strategies and visions into reality

Personality/Brand Character — Ambitious achiever ~ Visionary ~ Lead Conductor ~ Self-Assured ~ Optimist

Value you provide — ~ I influence others with ideas, plans & actions that yield results ~ I constantly learn, evaluate and optimize ~ I energetically tackle big goals

Differentiators — Consistently strong performance / High capacity for learning/growth/risk-taking / I lead people with heart

Exposure: Special project, 1:1s with mentors/sponsors, membership in industry organization, periodic LinkedIn posts

Figure 1.2.   Personal Brand Pyramid

being eliminated on a regular basis. Therefore, it is wise to think about the types of experiences you want to have. Career advancement doesn't always come in the form of a promotion. Sometimes experience, exposure, and lateral moves are the best career accelerators.

Step 2: Define Your Target Audience
Who are the influencers that need to understand who you are and how you uniquely add value? Who do you work with on a regular basis? This is the audience where you hone your skills, establish trust, and produce results. Who can provide feedback on your strengths and blind spots? Who do you want to work for in the future? All these parties make up your target audience.

Step 3: Define Your Purpose
Why do you exist, in the context of your professional endeavors? This statement can be inspired by your Product or "I am . . ." statement. This purpose should motivate, inspire, and be authentic to you.

Step 4: Capture Your Personality or Brand Character Attributes
Using the core values and strengths from your Personal Brand Audit, identify words or short phrases that embody the essence of your personality.

Step 5: Define the Value You Provide
In our careers, we get paid to produce results. What difference do you make in your organization? When you think about your "I am . . ." statement, what benefit does that have for others?

Step 6: Clarify Your Points of Differentiation
Use the content from your Personal Brand Audit to populate this section.

Step 7: Define Points of Exposure
Using the promotion and placement answers from your four Ps, define where and how you will get exposure to other people as well as channels that can reinforce your brand and become a champion for you.

Finally, after completing both tools, review the content of the Personal Brand Pyramid and determine if your purpose, brand character, value, and differentiators are aligned with your target role or experience. You can do this through personal reflection, observation, or consulting others who are familiar with what it takes to accomplish those achievements. If there isn't congruence between who you are at your core, how you show up to the world, and your aspirations, you have more work and soul-searching to do. If there is alignment, then you have just made a powerful investment in self-awareness that will enable you to be a more authentic, self-confident leader.

EMOTIONAL INTELLIGENCE INSIGHTS

1. Know thyself.
You are fearfully and wonderfully made with gifts, talents, perspectives, and experiences unlike anyone else in the entire world. When you're clear about your purpose, natural strengths, what doesn't come naturally to you, motivations, pain points, and triggers, you can operate more powerfully in the world and your organization. No one can define you better than you can.

"You're the architect of your career."

2. Bring your whole self to work, but be selective with what you share.
The world isn't ready for *all* your greatness, life experiences, or quirks.

"Be authentic enough to be true to yourself without losing yourself."

This requires managing your impulses. You can't say and do everything that comes to mind, especially in the work setting. Many organizations have "long memories," and it might come back to haunt you. Remember, you never have to apologize for what you *don't* say.

3. Dress for the job you want, not the job you have.

The essence of a "brand" is what you stand for in the hearts and minds of your target audience. At work, this audience includes your manager, direct and indirect leaders, peers, and direct reports. When you consistently perform at the next level and you look and act the part according to the people who matter, you position yourself for elevation.

"The time to start acting like a 'leader' is long before you get the title."

4. Instability reflects poorly on your capabilities.

The average hiring manager spends less than thirty seconds reviewing a résumé. If you've bounced around from company to company every few years throughout a ten-plus-year career, it's an immediate red flag. There might be a "fatal flaw" that creates more risk than reward for a company and manager. Solicit candid feedback about your strengths and opportunities, understand others' perspectives, then adapt your approach for longer staying power in a role or company. When you do seek new opportunities, vet the company, culture, and most important, the hiring manager.

"Ensure a mutual fit before you say yes *to a job."*

5. Perception is reality.

Often, there is a contradiction between how we see ourselves and how other people view us. Other people's perceptions, whether accurate or not, are their reality.

"Ask for feedback, then seek to understand,
but not obsess over, how you're viewed."

When soliciting feedback, include colleagues from work, home, and extracurricular activities, since you show different aspects of who you are in different settings. Then, work intentionally to close perception gaps that hurt your personal and professional brand.

6. Feedback is a gift that others don't have to give.

Here's a secret . . . most managers hesitate to give candid, constructive feedback. Why? Because it's difficult choosing the right words that will strike the balance of being insightful, empathetic, and motivational to the employee. Nonetheless, it's better to hear the feedback than to be ignorant.

> *"Interrupting others and defending yourself are sure ways to stop getting feedback that could make the difference between your being successful or stuck."*

7. The common denominator might be you.

If you seem to have an issue with nearly every manager, team, or company you work for or with, the issue might be you.

> *"We all have blind spots."*

Blind spots are characteristics that are known to others but oblivious to us. If you are committed to a prosperous career where people want to work with you, seek honest feedback, do some soul-searching, and make changes that result in a win–win for you and others. You'll be better because of it.

8. Quantify your impact, not your activities.

> *"Tasks, roles, and responsibilities are necessary but meaningless without tangible results."*

Goals are meant to be achieved, but sometimes unanticipated obstacles get in the way. Engage others to help address challenges and drive toward the goal of progress. Articulate the role you played in achieving these quantifiable results within quarterly check-ins, year-end reviews, on your résumé, and during interviews. Doing so will build your reputation, increase your value inside and outside of the organization, lead to greater retention, and increase your income.

9. Say *yes* to the invite.

While it may disrupt your routine and push you out of your comfort zone, lunch, happy hours, employee affinity group activities, charitable events, and work travel yield dividends. Socializing outside of work expands your network, and you'll be amazed what you learn about people, relationships and alliances, key initiatives, and the organization itself. When you're asked to take on a new role or special project, say *yes*. You'll endear yourself to influential leaders by appealing to their interests and priorities.

"When you make their priority your priority, you can both win."

10. I'm ready for the next level. Now what?
It's an exhilarating feeling to be promoted, but be sure you're not just chasing a title.

"Getting promoted before you're ready can backfire."

You know that you're ready for the next level of leadership when:

- You're able to juggle multiple demands with ease and time to spare.
- You see opportunities and build consensus for ideas and suggestions.
- Your work is consistently recognized as being stellar.
- People come to you for advice, guidance, and coaching.
- Your boss regularly assigns additional projects to you.

After talking with your manager and mentors, seek internal opportunities and explore external opportunities to assess your market value, provide a point of contrast, and enable negotiation leverage.

· 2 ·

Your Boss Isn't the Enemy

*H*ave you ever heard the phrase, "People don't leave their company, they leave their boss"? Like a marriage, some days working for a boss will feel like a mountaintop experience, and other days may leave you wondering if you can last one more day. However, the relationship with your direct manager is one of the most important relationships you need to advance your career because your manager influences your job performance rating, salary, and professional brand. If your manager won't vouch for you as you move to another role, let alone for a promotion, it creates doubt in the hiring manager's mind. While this isn't a showstopper, it does create more barriers for you to overcome.

I used to hold managers and others in authority to a higher standard, as if they had achieved a more perfect state of being, but a title doesn't make you invincible, flawless, or less imperfect. Titles bring more attention, focus, and judgment from more people across the organization. Therefore, it's in the best interest of the manager to acknowledge their strengths, weaknesses, insecurities, and emotions and for employees to do the same. Empathy and organizational awareness are the foundation for building a solid working relationship with your manager.

Leaders are stretched in many directions with many people they answer to. The accountability magnifies the higher up you go in an organization. People often complain about CEO compensation being too high. According to the 2018 Equilar Associated Press CEO Pay Study, median total compensation, including salary, bonus, stock and options, deferred compensation, benefits, and perks, for US S&P 500 CEOs totaled $11.7 million.[1] This is more money than most people will ever see in their lifetime. On the other hand, CEOs of Fortune 500 companies also face more responsibility and stress than most people will ever experience. While very few people will rise to the level of CEO, there are some parallels that are true for leaders at all levels.

There are multiple stakeholders that leaders are accountable to, affected by, and/or trying to influence, whether intentionally or unintentionally, including

- **Their manager.** You can't get around having to answer to someone with greater authority than you. Even CEOs and self-made entrepreneurs have a boss—the board of directors and customers, respectively. If the board becomes dissatisfied with the performance of you or your company and customers stop buying your products and services, you could eventually get ousted or go out of business. Based on the natural dynamics of power, your manager will always have a greater say than you do. Their opinions will matter more, their influence will be greater, and their decisions will have greater impact. Therefore, managing this critical relationship is paramount to successful performance that leads to career advancement.
- **Their manager's peers.** This is equivalent to relationships with siblings, only with higher stakes the higher you are in the organization. Each peer is vying for approval of their manager by demonstrating their unique value and delivering against their goals and objectives. However, when peers are competitive with one another, can't get along, and don't work well together, it creates a strained relationship between them as well as with your two-up boss. Therefore, it's incumbent on your manager to build strong collaborative relationships with their manager's other direct reports and with other peers across the organization.
- **Their direct reports.** Good managers get to know each of their direct reports—their strengths, opportunity areas, developmental needs, goals, and motivations. They develop attainable goals that accomplish the organization's objectives, build self-esteem in the employee, and help them attain the professional goals they've set for themselves. In addition to check-ins, at least once a year, good managers provide written feedback and engage in a dialogue on employees' performance. This is best accomplished by combining their personal observations with feedback

from others. With these examples, a good manager will deliver feedback in a tailored way that the employee can receive, then provide specific recommendations for continued development. Often, this type of engagement by a manager with direct reports isn't specifically rewarded in annual performance reviews or salary increases. Instead, the benefits are realized when people on their teams achieve the stated performance goals, are motivated to give their best efforts, and want to work for that leader. All these attributes build a stronger brand for your manager, which will help them increase their influence and advance their career.

- **Your peers.** The same dynamic that exists with your manager's peers also exists with your peers. Trust me that no manager wants to get in between quarreling teammates. It's an unwelcomed distraction that is mentally exhausting. That's why so many managers avoid addressing people-related conflicts head-on. Do yourself a favor—make your manager's job easier by getting along with your peers and working together to accomplish the job that needs to be done.
- **Their team.** A large part of any leader's role is developing strategy, especially the higher one rises in an organization. The best strategies aren't on paper alone but the ones that are realized through execution by teams of people within and outside of your function. Therefore, a leader must drive clarity in goals, objectives, action plans, metrics, and timing to realize the strategy.

Along the journey, there will be unanticipated roadblocks that arise. A great leader addresses these barriers and demonstrates organizational awareness by listening to their teams, understanding the problems, engaging in a dialogue, inviting recommendations from those closest to the work, then leveraging the power of their network to influence others, resolve conflicts, and overcome these barriers. Sometimes members of your team feel dissatisfied, overworked, or frustrated, or there may be a risk of attrition. Sometimes there's a benefit to getting fresh talent on a team; however, losing regrettable talent has a ripple effect on goal achievement, team culture, and the brand of the team's leaders. Therefore, taking steps to fully engage employees, however far down in the organization they may be, is critical for leaders.

- **The broader organization.** The higher you go, the more eyes there are watching you. It sounds a little creepy, but it's uncanny how much people are watching you in an organization. I recall hearing someone describe what it was like to be a newly hired CEO. Prior to coming to that company, he dressed fashionably, wearing tailored suits, engraved cufflinks, and designer shoes. He also drove a high-end European luxury car and parked in a reserved spot in the front of the parking lot with his name on the placard. With back-to-back meetings, there was rarely time to spend with many employees or engage them in the hallways. Instead, his exposure was limited to a small group of direct reports and peers.

  When his 90-day check-in occurred, he was stunned by the feedback. The board was more than pleased with his work performance; however, they expressed concern around his "fit," a nebulous term describing how well someone adapts to the organizational culture. Committed to his success in this role and at the company, he sprang into action.

  The CEO solicited broad-based feedback to increase organizational awareness. He discovered that his personal brand was described as impersonal and haughty. So he adapted some of his behaviors and brand image, starting with his attire. Instead of wearing designer suits every day, he expanded his wardrobe to include button-down shirts, sweater vests, and slacks. He kept his premium parking spot, but instead of driving his luxury car to work, he convinced the board to provide a company car. He chose an all-American, unpretentious Buick. Finally, he began scheduling quarterly donut and coffee chats for employees across functions and levels. These small steps transformed his brand image into an in-touch leader that people wanted to follow.

  Consider the attributes of emotional intelligence that he employed:

  ○ Organizational awareness and self-awareness: The unexpected feedback helped to increase sensitivity to the perceptions and feelings of others, which increased his own self-awareness.
  ○ Emotional self-control: He embraced the board's feedback and maintained his composure instead of becoming defensive

or expecting that an organization would completely adapt itself to his style. After all, the organization was there before he arrived and would continue to sustain long after he was gone.

○ Adaptability and achievement orientation: He continued to drive his luxury car outside of work and dress the way he felt most comfortable in other settings. While at work, however, he adapted to the company culture because he knew it would be one less barrier to achieving his goals and objectives. Plus, the bonus benefit was an improved brand reputation.

○ Influence and inspirational leadership: Becoming more approachable from a distance and in more formal and informal settings furthered the CEO's influence and inspirational leadership. People follow and do business with people they like. Winning over both the hearts and the minds of people accelerates what can be achieved.

While the details of this situation may not apply to your circumstance, I hope you can see how big of a shadow you cast just by virtue of a managerial title and responsibilities.

- **Their family and loved ones.** Many leaders work together with their spouses, significant others, and other family members to provide a particular lifestyle for their families. Taking on risk, changing companies, and relocating cities are a bit easier when there's only one person involved. However, when family members are involved, these changes have a domino effect on others. While it may not be at the top of your mind daily, during times of change, disruption, and dissatisfaction, your manager is considering the needs of and impact to their family and loved ones.
- **Themselves.** Last but not least, your manager must answer to themselves. Are they accomplishing the business objectives? Do they have credibility within the organization? Are they on track to achieve their professional goals? Are they happy and satisfied? These are just a few considerations included in their ongoing journey with self-awareness.

Once I led a team during an acquisition. While some acquisitions can be "bolted on" to the acquiring company's operation, others require deep integration. In my case, both legacy companies had duplicate teams, functions, and even customers. With that much redundancy, it's inevitable that significant change was on the horizon.

I was young in my corporate career and naively believed that the acquired company was obligated to adapt to my acquiring company's culture, norms, and operational practices. The organizational changes resulted in gaining both a new boss and general manager from the acquired company, conflict between functions, and an array of emotions. It didn't take long for me to realize that my lack of self-awareness and self-management were having a negative impact on my direct reports and team. I was experiencing the same anxiety, vulnerability, uncertainty, excitement, pride, and grief that my teams were also feeling. However, as leaders, we are not only responsible for ourselves but also for our teams.

Since that time, I've experienced more acquisitions—always on the acquiring end—and have put these emotional intelligence insights into practice. First, I get in touch with my own feelings and raw emotions. Second, I think through how my teams might be feeling. This comes through observation, indirect commentary, dialogue, and listening. Third, I carefully think through the message I will share with the team, which usually balances showing empathy for how they might be feeling, demonstrating vulnerability by expressing how I'm feeling, and leaving them with a touch of inspiration for a better, brighter future. The approach to combine self-awareness, empathy, and organizational awareness can help you become an inspirational leader.

When you consider your manager's task to manage these wildly diverse stakeholders, deliver business results, and build and nurture a productive team and organizational culture, it's no wonder why pressure cooker environments can often lead to stress and other mental health issues. There's a lot riding on the decisions, behaviors, and outcomes of leaders who work long hours, manage unpredictability, deal with ambiguity, and try to be a role model for others.

Because managers are human too, they are prone to many of the same challenges that non-managers face. For example, according to the National Institute of Mental Health, approximately one in five adults in the United States—46.6 million in 2017, or 18.9 percent—experiences mental illness in a given year.[2] Depression is the leading cause of disability worldwide and is a major contributor to the global burden of disease.[3] However, a recent study showed that employed people with prestigious jobs, higher salaries, and higher status who sought help for depression showed poorer response to treatment and higher rates of treatment-resistant depression.[4] These executives failed to respond to at least two antidepressant regimes—a change of antidepressants, shifting from antidepressant to psychotherapy or vice versa, or the combination of both treatments.[5] By the end of the study, only one in six patients from the higher-status group achieved remission from an episode of depression. In contrast, middle-level and low-level occupations achieved remission among one in four.[6] This study was conducted among patients who sought treatment; however, a 2010 study found that about half of Americans with major depressive disorder did not get any treatment.[7] While we are not responsible for our managers' mental and emotional health, we can do our part by making their jobs easier—deliver results, be accountable, avoid surprises, help solve their problems and pain points, advance their agendas, and speak well of them to others.

The sources of workplace stress are diverse for leaders and employees alike. According to *Psych Central*,[8] these stresses include

- Life events
- Daily hassles
- Conflict management
- Communication styles
- Personality traits
- Perception factors
- Role ambiguity
- Role conflict
- Excessive work
- Decreased autonomy
- Lack of support

Dealing with a bad manager, or a good manager having a bad day, can be tough. Inevitably, there will be conflict, and in many cases, it's not personal and your boss isn't the enemy. There may be mindsets, motivations, and fears you can visibly observe, hear, and experience; however, there are usually invisible issues below the iceberg that affect their words, actions, and behaviors (see figure 2.1). Engaging in conversation, asking questions that seek to understand, and listening attentively can provide context clues about what concerns your manager, which leads to greater empathy. For example, if your manager keeps repeating something, name-drops their boss or another person of influence, or shows more intense emotions or a different tone of voice than normal, that's a context clue that the subject is probably important to them. Helping to solve your manager's problems is a key building block to a strong relationship.

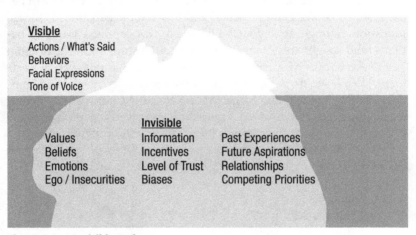

Visible
Actions / What's Said
Behaviors
Facial Expressions
Tone of Voice

Invisible

Values	Information	Past Experiences
Beliefs	Incentives	Future Aspirations
Emotions	Level of Trust	Relationships
Ego / Insecurities	Biases	Competing Priorities

Figure 2.1.   Invisible Iceberg

On more than one occasion, I've observed, managed, and mentored employees who interpreted their manager's words, actions, and behaviors as a personal assault. Without question, there are some people who have no business being managers and intentionally mistreat employees. However, in many cases, leaders are doing their best to juggle several balls in the air, and although it sounds harsh, they may not have given their employees much thought. When situations arise that could lead to a misunderstanding, in-person dialogue, or a phone conversation with someone who is geographically dispersed, is my preferred style of conflict resolution. Conversations reduce the potential for defensiveness and provide an opportunity to establish common ground.

Even after engaging in dialogue, there are times when your manager will make a decision that you disagree with. If they're steering the ship in a specific direction, as difficult as it may be, and if the decision isn't unethical or illegal, sometimes your best course of action is to "get in the boat, shut up, and row." Expressing unwavering disapproval, concern, or resistance will do more harm than good. If you can't live with the decision, it may be time to step off the boat altogether.

In my experience, one of the biggest frustrations with managers of high achievers is pitching new ideas. Innovation is the lifeblood of any sustainable organization. Innovation includes identifying new ways of driving efficiency, effectiveness, and speed. It can also mean introducing new products and services that deliver against unmet needs and either decrease costs, grow revenue, and/or increase profit. However, according to a 2017 Innovation Matters study by PA Consulting Group based in London, among the senior executives surveyed from around the globe, 50 percent do not believe their leaders fully display the vision and passion needed to make innovation happen.[9] Let's face it—innovation is fraught with risk, which can translate to fear. People ask, or think about, the following types of questions: What if it fails? Do I understand or believe in it enough to personally advocate for this change? What if it disrupts my power or influence? Can we afford to think long-term when we're tasked with delivering short-term results and financial targets? What if we waste valuable resources and kill projects before they launch? Do we have the resilience to bounce back from failure?

Despite these concerns, there are a few reasons why organizations, teams, managers, and high achievers shouldn't be complacent or satisfied with the status quo.

- If the competition is innovating and you're stagnant, you are falling behind. Technology is making it easier for competitors to enter and disrupt the market. Think about how Netflix disrupted Blockbuster Video or how Uber disrupted the taxi industry. Anticipating change and embracing technology and the digital revolution will help reduce the odds of your organization becoming the next dying, irrelevant brand. Disruptive innovation is discussed further in chapter 7.
- Customers have more choices today than ever. In the digital age, they're also more connected globally. Delighting existing customers to maintain loyalty is much more efficient than attracting a new customer or winning back a lapsed customer.
- Attracting and retaining top talent will be difficult for organizations unwilling to consider new ways of operating, especially

since millennial workers (ages 24 to 39 in 2020) are the largest generation in the labor force, representing 56 million U.S. workers (35 percent of the workforce).[10] Many of these employees are college-educated and have lofty aspirations with the motivation to make a tangible impact to meaningful work.

Since most people are wired to maintain the status quo and resist change, innovators will always be a minority group—they are fewer in number, less powerful, and have the burden of proof to convince influencers and decision makers that the current course of action is insufficient. Making a believer out of your manager is one of the most critical steps you can take to advance your ideas. Here are some strategies to get your manager and others on board with your ideas.

1. **Build a business case.** What is the problem and for whom? What's the risk of the status quo? What are the rational and emotional benefits? What are the alternatives? (See chapter 4 for more guidance on influence.)

2. **Align the idea** with the strategic imperatives of the company and/or the mindset, motivations, and fears of your manager. Will your idea help advance the agendas of the company and your manager or mitigate risks? Will it solve a problem that is important to your manager? Will it reflect positively on them? Does it align with their incentives and performance objectives? Consider your manager's iceberg. You must understand the key stakeholders' positions and potential barriers.

    Alignment significantly increases the odds of your idea being considered and adopted because it positions you as an "insider." It also reduces the risk of being perceived as a divergent outsider who can't be trusted or whose idea is threatening. When you paint the picture of what the future could be, use words like "we," "our," and "us." It sends a subtle message that reinforces the benefits not just for you but for the whole.

3. **Enlist the support of cross-functional peers.** Showing that the idea has been vetted and has the unanimous support of multiple people who your manager respects and values builds credibility and momentum for a stronger, more persuasive idea.

4. **Be willing to compromise.** Innovation is a series of negotiations of what's attractive, feasible, justifiable, and can be supported. Give up the notion that the first draft of your idea is the final masterpiece. Proactively invite suggestions, probes, and concerns with your manager. It will show that you're committed, but not emotionally attached, to your ideas or pride of ownership. Showing flexibility and a reasoned response will enhance your influence.

5. **Be patient yet persistent.** Influence is shaped by consistency, persistence, and unanimity. Sometimes you may have a great idea at an inopportune time. Remain steadfast in your quest for change that will benefit the organization and its customers. If you've pitched an idea and gotten a no or not now response, don't fret. Put your idea on the proverbial shelf and revisit it when the time is right.

6. **Know when to call it quits.** Some of the best leaders are clear in their communication, but many are less direct. If you experience the following tactics, it could mean that your manager is not supportive of your idea:

   • Shifting the subject
   • Ignoring
   • Casting doubt
   • Discounting credibility
   • Listing risks and barriers
   • Defending their position or self-interests

Their lack of support can cause you to feel dismayed and rejected. Grieve for a moment, then regroup and refocus your energy on what can be accomplished and supported.

As you build your leadership acumen and advance your career, I encourage you to adopt an enterprise mindset. Enterprise thinking is the practice of considering the entire enterprise in decision making, not just a given group or department. Consider the various stakeholders listed earlier in the chapter. Enterprise thinking will help you develop into a more well-rounded, empathetic leader whose concerns extend beyond your own self-serving needs and desires.

Developing an enterprise mindset requires curiosity—asking questions and learning about other parts of the business beyond your siloed business unit, department, function, or team in formal and informal settings alike. Many organizations are matrixed, which requires a higher degree of interdependency and collaboration across functions, geographies, systems, customers, divisions, and business units. When you engage a diverse group of stakeholders, you gain insights that can ultimately strengthen your idea and address potential barriers. Plus, your relevance can increase among people with interests and incentives different than your own, which enables more robust networking conversations and enhances your brand reputation as an influential, in-touch leader.

EMOTIONAL INTELLIGENCE INSIGHTS

11. Understand their mindset, motivations, and fears.
There are very few organizations in which people can make unilateral decisions. Therefore, the importance of influential leadership cannot be understated. To effectively influence your manager and others, you must understand their

- **Mindset**—What are their values, priorities, actual and desired reputation, strategies, and goals? What is their current situation, and how could that context influence their decisions?
- **Motivations**—What's their personal and professional why? What are their desires, success metrics, and incentives, and who are their key influencers?
- **Fears**—What are their most pressing pain points and fears? Who are their detractors? Do they need to "write a new story" to create a more favorable brand image?

"When you understand mindset, motivations, and fears,
you can empathize with your leaders, work intentionally to help
them accomplish their goals, and increase your influence."

12. Strive to make your manager look good.
Managers are imperfect, just like us. Sometimes, however, that imperfection can lead to an employee's frustration.

"Creating a healthy rapport with your manager enables you to resolve conflict privately so you can help them shine publicly."

Aligning your strategies, goals, deliverables, words, and behaviors to your manager's mindset and motivations will make them look good and feel good too.

13. Some situations are above your paygrade.
Leaders are under tremendous pressure to deliver results, strengthen their brand, and navigate ever-present organizational politics full of competing priorities and competing agendas. Sometimes leaders make decisions employees don't understand, agree with, or fully appreciate.

"There are often factors 'below the iceberg' you may never know about."

Sometimes your role is to contribute to the decision; other times, decisions are made for you.

14. Extend grace.
We all have off days. Because of human nature, moods, and emotions, our words, tone of voice, actions, and behaviors can sometimes be misinterpreted.

"Be difficult to offend."

Try not to add meaning to words—listen to what others say and accept it at face value. Assume good intent and extend grace. After some time has passed, if you're still bothered about a situation, have a conversation with the sole purpose of helping your manager to be great.

When you've built a foundation of trust, consistent performance, and mutual respect, it leaves an opening for valuable feedback on the impact we have on others and, sometimes, its unintended consequences.

Be selective with how often you have this dialogue so that you're not labeled a "problem child." Ensure your motivations are for your manager's benefit and not a gotcha moment. There are few, if any, upsides of making your manager look and feel bad.

15. Forgive frequently.
Harboring feelings of resentment has a damaging effect on your engagement and productivity, and it's toxic for relationships and the team culture. It's difficult for employees who feel like they're walking on

eggshells. It's equally uncomfortable for leaders because even more is at stake, including the domino effect on the rest of the team, the business, and their personal reputation. If you can't resolve the conflict internally, bring the disagreement out in the open to deescalate the situation and seek a solution everyone can accept.

"Forgive others because not doing so creates a heavy burden for you."

• 3 •

What You Need to Lead but Won't
Learn in Business School

*N*o matter what industry you work in, if you're a leader of people, you're in the people business. Without people to execute the strategies you craft and the plans you define, there would be no industry or business. Therefore, it is critical to study people just as much, or more than, you study functional subjects.

Master of business administration (MBA) degrees provide a cross-functional foundation of business fundamentals, including finance, accounting, economics, law, ethics, marketing, management, operations, and human resources. The curriculum is usually a combination of individual assignments, research papers, group assignments, and case studies.

Group assignments are particularly useful because they force you to engage with peers from diverse backgrounds, functions, geographies, and experiences. Your task is to complete an assignment together; however, in both work, school, and life, everyone doesn't always pull their weight. The standard of what's acceptable can vary from person to person. Sometimes having multiple A-type personalities in a group leads to conflict. It's a good primer for eventual on-the-job management, but it won't fully prepare you for the rigors of leadership.

The case study method is another strategy many business schools leverage to prepare their students. Based on real situations confronting businesses, nonprofits, and government organizations, these written summaries provide an overview of the situation, people involved, and visual aids such as charts, graphs, and tables. The student identifies the problem, conducts analysis, explores alternative courses of action, weighs pros and cons, and provides a recommendation. While the written case contains constraints, the information is incomplete, which makes each case dynamic and complex, just like real business and organizational issues we face daily.

The professors, who have more detailed information than the written case study, lead students through rich dialogue to exchange ideas, share countering and defending points, analyze issues, exercise judgment, see situations from different perspectives, and make difficult decisions for answers that aren't always clear and conclusive. At the end of the conversation, the professor shares the real-life conclusion and results. This provides students greater opportunity for hindsight reflection in the context of the prior dialogue, their own conclusions, and the team's recommendation. As invaluable as this experience is for students, it is also inadequate for the true rigors of leadership and leading people.

When it comes to leading people, experience is the best teacher. There's no getting around it, and, in my opinion, it's not something that can be mastered because life is dynamic. People change. Situations change. Priorities change. Perspectives change. Emotions change. To thrive as a leader, we must demonstrate agility, that is, moving quickly and easily toward a desired end. Despite never-ending changes, there are some time-tested strategies I leverage when I'm new to a team, welcoming a new team member, getting a new manager, joining up with a cross-functional business partner, and creating and maintaining healthy relationships and a team culture, which are shared in the balance of this chapter.

WHEN YOU'RE NEW TO A ROLE

Demonstrating strong performance in your role is the first step to building credibility and gaining the respect of your teams, peers, and leaders. Prior to starting a new role, read as much about the business, performance, and team as you can, for as far back as you can. This could include annual reports, organizational strategies and priorities, business reviews, presentations, research reports, customer feedback, project briefings, competitive reviews, organizational charts, employee feedback, and performance reviews. If there's an opportunity to transition from your predecessor, take advantage of that opportunity to learn as much as you can about the business, strategy, operational plans, people, opportunities, and challenges. Ask many questions seeking to understand and not judge. Validate your understanding of the business based on your independent research. If you can meet with your predecessor at the start of your role and again within your first thirty days once you've had some firsthand experience, that will set you up for greater success.

During your first ninety days, you should be like a sponge, absorbing as much information and insight as possible. Besides periodic questions aimed at deepening your understanding of the organization, business, people, and processes, most of your time should be spent listening. While different people have varying learning techniques, I prefer creating a binder with printed documents that I can write on, highlight, and make notes in with key aha moments, questions, comments, or ideas.

Capture your hypotheses, ideas, and observations in a journal. As you meet more people and learn about the business, you can validate or invalidate your hypotheses. Forming conclusions and making decisions too early in your role can be disastrous. So it is very important that your tone of voice communicate exploration, not decisiveness or judgment. These validated hypotheses will become the basis of your future vision, strategies, and/or operational plans.

I've built my career in product and brand management. While your industry may differ, here is an example of my transition checklist when I'm starting a new role or onboarding my successor.

Transition Checklist

Strategy and Initiatives
- Review strategies and plans.
- Conduct a landscape assessment: with a business review, the five Cs (customer, competitor, channel, company, category), and a SWOT analysis (strengths, weaknesses, opportunities, and threats).
- Review active innovation and cost improvement projects.
- Review innovation pipeline and ideas for growth and cost reduction.
- Ask what the team should start/stop/continue to every person you meet.

Learn the Business and Build Relationships
- Do a portfolio review—the most recent year, over the past two to three years, and as far back as beneficial.
- Get added to the distribution list for standard reports.
- Secure training for critical systems and processes.
- Define key relationships (name, title, role, contact info, and manager's name) with key functions (HR, manufacturing, sourcing, finance, sales, inventory, quality, regulatory, etc.).
- Engage with manufacturing teams and visit facilities (if applicable).
- Conduct onboarding meetings with all the aforementioned people and teams.
- Conduct business and functional reviews where the team presents the business to you. It's an excellent opportunity for you to quickly learn the business and get firsthand experience with the people on the team.
- Exchange physical and digital files.

Engage with the Team
- Conduct 1:1 meetings with direct reports and/or extended team/functional partners.
- Conduct and/or participate in team and customer/external meetings.
- Get plugged into established meeting cadences.
- Set meeting cadences for new direct reports, team, and cross-functional business partners.

Sales/Finance
- Confirm actual and budgeted revenue, profit, and expenses.
- Review historical financial performance—actual versus budget and current versus prior year.
- Review building blocks, sales pipeline, risks, and opportunities.
- Actively engage with the sales team across touchpoints (i.e., phone, email, in-person, team meetings).

Marketing
- Deeply understand target customer audience and "bullseye" target, which is the audience where your business has the strongest affinity for the products and services.
- Understand size of prize (revenue potential) and right to win (points of difference and advantages why your business can win with the target audience).
- Understand the customer journey, including what they're seeking, what influences them, and how they make decisions.
- Review market research, insights, and reports; take notes and identify questions, hypotheses, and ideas to explore further with the team.
- Review marketing positioning, objectives, plans, commercial messaging, budget, calendar, content, and historical performance.

Talent
- Define business objectives; ensure these objectives are clear to the team and cascaded in individual performance goals.
- Establish and/or confirm performance objectives, timelines, and milestones.
- For every direct report and their direct reports, at a minimum, review their résumé and/or talent card and have a conversation about their individual motivations, professional goals, Top 5 CliftonStrengths results, and communication preferences.

Leadership Credo
Sharing a summary of who you are as a leader, what you believe, how those values and beliefs guide your actions, and how you operate demonstrates self-awareness and authenticity. Creating a simple "playbook" helps to ease anxiety, build trust, and establish expectations, which significantly accelerates relationship development with your new team. There is no right or wrong way to create and share this snapshot. Leaders take many approaches, with varying content that can include the following:

- Values, principles, and beliefs that are important to you, and why.
- Quotes, metaphors, stories, or role models that relate to or illustrate your values and principles.
- Who and what you value outside of work (i.e., family/family picture, pets, volunteer activities, hobbies). This humanizes you as a leader, provides more opportunities for connection, and helps you be more approachable.
- Communication style and preferences.

Johnson & Johnson has one of the most revered credos of any corporation. These values are a moral compass that guide decision making and challenge their employees to put the needs and well-being of the people they serve first.

According to the Johnson & Johnson website,[1] Robert Wood Johnson, former chairman from 1932 to 1963 and a member of the company's founding family, crafted the company credo himself in 1943, just before Johnson & Johnson became a publicly traded company. This was long before anyone ever heard of "corporate social responsibility." They believe it's been a recipe for business success. Johnson & Johnson is one of only a handful of companies that has flourished through more than a century of change, which is proof of the influence its credo has had on its success.

Our Credo

We believe our first responsibility is to the patients, doctors and nurses, to mothers and fathers and all others who use our products and services. In meeting their needs everything we do must be of high quality. We must constantly strive to provide value, reduce our costs and maintain reasonable prices. Customers' orders must be serviced promptly and accurately. Our business partners must have an opportunity to make a fair profit.

We are responsible to our employees who work with us throughout the world. We must provide an inclusive work environment where each person must be considered as an individual. We must respect their diversity and dignity and recognize their merit. They must have a sense of security, fulfillment and purpose in their jobs. Compensation must be fair and adequate and working conditions clean, orderly and safe. We must support the health and well-being of our employees and help them fulfill their family and other personal responsibilities. Employees must feel free to make suggestions and complaints. There must be equal opportunity for employment, development and advancement for those qualified. We must provide highly capable leaders and their actions must be just and ethical.

We are responsible to the communities in which we live and work and to the world community as well. We must help people be healthier by supporting better access and care in more places around the world. We must be good citizens—support good works and charities, better health and education, and bear our fair share of taxes. We must maintain in good order the property we are privileged to use, protecting the environment and natural resources.

Our final responsibility is to our stockholders. Business must make a sound profit. We must experiment with new ideas. Research must be carried on, innovative programs developed, investments made for the future and mistakes paid for. New equipment must be purchased, new facilities provided, and new products launched. Reserves must be created to provide for adverse times. When we operate according to these principles, the stockholders should realize a fair return.[2]

Here are additional examples of leaders' credos and leadership snapshots.

Leadership Credo Example A   These are the values that I hold to when leading myself and that I look for in other people. I will expect my leaders, my peers, my team, and my employees to challenge me when my behavior does not reflect these values. I will reflect on my actions to ensure I follow my heart. I acknowledge that over time, my understanding of what I value most may change, and I will be honest with myself when I recognize changes.

Openness—I will openly share information about myself with anyone who needs to know except for information about my family that only my friends and family need to know. I will openly share information about my work with anyone who needs to know except for information about my work that my employer has instructed me not to share. If I don't share information with others, it is because it is not my information to share, as it falls into one of the exceptions above or I don't have information to share.

Integrity—I will always act honestly and fairly. I believe that rules are to be followed and myths are to be dispelled. Holding a known myth up as a rule has about as much integrity as knowingly breaking rules.

Accountability and Responsibility—I will accept and acknowledge my responsibilities, personal actions, and outputs. I will take ownership of my own success and work through my failures. I expect the same of others to whom I have entrusted responsibility through appointment, assignment, or delegation.

Loyalty—I will support my employees, my team, my colleagues, and my organization in achieving their goals. I am not successful if I do not support those around me in achieving their success. I will defend the reputations of those who cannot defend themselves or who are not present to defend themselves. I value when others do the same.

Personal Development—I will continue to learn and seek new opportunities that may be outside my profession. I will encourage and assist others in developing and improving themselves. I believe that every individual is solely responsible and accountable for their own learning and development. I believe blaming others for failing to teach or train is dodging your personal responsibility.

Challenge—I will continue to seek and accept opportunities that take me outside my comfort zone. I will seek out and bust myths. Without challenge, there is no risk of failure, and consequently, there is no opportunity for personal or corporate learning.

Leadership Credo Example B
- Do everything with integrity.
- Be committed to your work.
- Encourage and help people.
- Respect others and their opinions.
- Be open-minded.
- Be calm in times of change/distress.
- Value every person's differences and skills.
- Be honest with myself and others.
- Take risks—don't be afraid.
- Take constructive criticism.

- Learn how to implement change and develop new ideas.
- Listen to people's thoughts and opinions.
- Learn from mistakes.

Leadership Credo Example C
Introduction—originally from Columbus, Ohio; BA and MBA from Florida A&M University; eight years general management/brand management at Procter & Gamble; five years innovation/brand management at the Hershey Company; started at Cardinal Health in 2014.

- Likes
  - Spending time with my family (three children), attending church, and volunteering with my public service sorority.
  - Transforming insights, data, and intuition into actionable plans that deliver results.
  - Leading training, coaching others, and recruiting.
  - Global travel and ethnic foods.
- CliftonStrengths: Achiever, Strategic, Relator, Maximizer, Significance
  - Achiever + Strategic + Relator: I love to explore possibilities with teams, decide on a path, and go. There's nothing we can't accomplish together. Even if we fail, we'll be better for having tried.
  - Maximizer + Significance: I get joy when we go from good to great and make a meaningful impact on individuals, teams, and the business/organization.
  - Other Top 10 Strengths: Focus, Learner, Responsibility, Positivity, Arranger—I follow through on commitments, even if I have to sacrifice sleep or personal time.
- Pet Peeves
  - Indecisiveness; jumping into the details before understanding the big picture; lack of transparency and hidden agendas; passive-aggressive behavior.
  - "Lack of planning on your end does not necessitate an emergency on my part."
- Beliefs
  - The consumer/customer is "boss."

- Why not? Anything's possible! Challenge assumptions.
- Everyone can teach, and everyone can learn—"When you know better, you'll do better."
- Personal and professional growth is often accompanied by some level of discomfort.
- Personal Style—What You Can Expect from Me
  - Be accountable, set clear priorities, exhibit passion, and drive for results.
  - Invest in you—provide feedback, probe thinking/multiple lenses, ask your recommendation/rationale, value your opinion, praise/recognition.
  - Empower you—provide clarity on the goals, assign competent team members or provide guidance and resources to establish competency, and give room to make mistakes.
  - Showcase your work with executives, praise and recognition.
  - Trust, honesty, and transparency.
  - To maintain work–life balance and have "thinking and working time"—when possible, I prefer to schedule meetings between 10 a.m. and 4 p.m. Sometimes I work best at night, so if you see an email from me in the wee hours, please know that there are no expectations of you to do the same. ☺
  - Honor vacation and paid time off.
- My Expectations—What I Expect from Direct Reports/Team Members
  - Think, don't just do—have a point of view and recommendation. Speak your mind in a respectful way; share context, details/nuances, pros/cons, other options considered.
  - Own your initiatives; help me understand what help/support you need.
  - Provide honest, timely feedback—what's working and what's not.
  - Develop your people.
  - No surprises.
- Communication Preferences
  - I work hard to be approachable and accessible—drop by (ask, "do you have a few minutes?"), call/text anytime, request time on calendar (with prior heads-up), avoid 12 to 1 p.m. lunchtime meetings.

- ○ Weekly leadership team meeting—What do you need me to know? What help do you need? What are you stuck on?
- ○ Monthly business unit update / Quarterly scorecard.
- ○ Send prereading at least twenty-four hours in advance before requesting feedback—printouts are helpful.
- ○ Limit email, to the extent possible, and leverage 4D approach—delete, delegate, do, and defer.

Once you have prepared your credo, share it with your direct reports and their teams in a single group setting as early in your tenure as possible, sometime between Day 1 and the end of your first thirty days. Be prepared to elaborate on why each of these values and beliefs are so important to you. Consider telling stories, which are especially powerful because they demonstrate vulnerability and emotional intelligence and can help create connections with your teams that translate to a more motivated workforce. Be sure your team has a hard and soft copy that they can reference in the future.

DAY 1 MEETING

On your first day, host a team meeting to get to know your team and for them to learn more about you. Chances are, if the announcement of your role has already been made, they will have done research and asked other people about you. This team meeting is your first opportunity to establish your personal brand and set the tone for your future engagement. Content for this meeting should include

- A brief personal and professional background introduction—where you're from, about your family, professional experiences.
- Why you accepted this role.
- What you are committed to for the team, business, organization, and culture.
- Address directly or indirectly the questions and concerns your team may have.
- Introductions from your team (name, role, and an interesting fact or some other icebreaker).

- Paint a picture of what the next few weeks will consist of. For example, this could include hosting 1:1 meetings with direct reports, individual skip-level meetings with team members deeper within your organization, coffee chats, and/or team meetings. Share any upcoming travel plans and how they can get in touch with you.
- Close with your optimism about working together as a new team.

In my quest to become a more inspirational leader, one time I tried something a little different. During our Day 1 introductory meeting, I gave each team member ten to fifteen minutes to write a short story about their life and origin. While it's a short period of time, writing it quickly enabled a more powerful, authentic experience. To set up the exercise, I played a ninety-second inspirational "Where I'm From" video of George Ella Lyon, the poet who inspired the exercise.[3] Here is the letter I shared in a 2016 Day 1 team meeting:

I am from . . .

I am from Joan and Richard Tucker, a social worker turned entrepreneur and Christian counselor mom, and a compassionate blue-collar dad whose recurring epilepsy challenged his profession in sales but didn't kill his spirit. The only grandchild of Betty Marie, whose wisdom and love of nearly ninety-eight years this July drew me back to my hometown of Columbus after a hiatus of education and career building for nearly twenty years.

Most people are surprised to learn that I'm an only child. Fiercely independent. A serial entrepreneur who started at the tender age of fourteen teaching piano to four-year-olds and eighty-year-olds alike. I am an explorer, a risk-taker, and a global traveler who loves to experience other cultures and understand other peoples' one-of-a-kind stories. This led me from class presidency in a public high school on the east side of Columbus down south to Florida A&M University, one of the largest Historically Black Colleges and Universities in the country.

Throughout my journey, passion, belief, and a willingness to be the change I wish to see has compelled me to lead national protests against inequitable educational policies and to spend countless hours leading and volunteering with young people to find their path to success.

I am a wife, who divorced and remarried my college sweetheart. I believe in restoration. I believe in transformation. Anything is possible.

God has called me to minister to others, but my first ministry is to my family and our three children.
    I work hard. I love hard. I play hard. I aspire to leave this world better for my having been here. And that is where I'm from.

Once people wrote their own "Where I'm From" stories, they read them aloud to the group. It was truly a moment of vulnerability—very productive in learning who people are, who and what shaped the person they've become, and the beginning formation of a healthy bond between individuals and as a team. Even people who had worked together for years learned something new about their teammates.

1:1 ONBOARDING MEETINGS

After the introductory team meeting, and within your first week on the job, host a one-hour join-up meeting with each of your direct reports. Within the first two months, host a thirty-minute 1:1 meeting with team members across multiple levels in your organization, along with your cross-functional team members. In preparation for each of these meetings, review where they sit in the organization chart, understand their individual roles and projects at a 30,000 feet level, and, if they are within your hierarchy and you have access, read their last performance review and résumé.

While they may be able to answer specific questions that you've gathered during your research, do your best to refrain from asking too many specific questions about the business, and instead focus 90 percent of the time on listening and getting to know your direct reports during this first meeting. This will be one of few meetings without a two-way dialogue, so take good notes. There will be plenty of time to get into the details of your new role, answer questions from your research, and get feedback on your hypotheses, early observations, and potential changes during future conversations. Here are the standard questions I ask during 1:1 onboarding meetings:

1. Tell me about your background.
   This should include their professional experiences, such as prior companies/organizations, prior assignments, and current roles

and responsibilities. Depending on their comfort level, they could also share about their family—if they're married, have children, grandchildren, nieces and nephews, and so on.

2. What motivates you?
This is very important to know and understand because it answers the age-old question—what's in it for me? These insights can be used to eventually lead, influence, and motivate them. For example, their motivations could be recognition, team wins, advancement, better ratings than peers, compensation, exposure, or being a role model, a provider for their family, or a trusted advisor. By giving your employees what they want and meeting their personal needs and motivations consistently over time, they are more likely to reciprocate by working hard to give you what you need to be successful.

One question I often ask is, "What are you most proud of in your career?" Not only do I appreciate accomplishments, their answer helps me understand what types of results and contributions get them excited.

3. What are your professional goals?
Employees aren't asked this question often, so it's refreshing when someone cares enough to ask. The answer to this question can have many benefits, including

- Understanding the level of their commitment to the role and/ or organization.
- Assessing their level of job satisfaction or dissatisfaction through what they say, their tone of voice, and other non-verbal cues.
- And most important, sending a message to your employee about your care and concern for their career.

Especially for employees classified as high potential or high performing, ask what support they need from you to be successful. While you don't need to overtly share their talent segmentation, asking this question signals that you're committed to investing in their continued success.

4. What should we start/stop/continue?

    This is a nonthreatening way to get candid feedback on what's going well and what's not going well with the business, team, and organization. Do your best to exhibit emotional self-control and refrain from jumping to conclusions or making promises you might not be able to keep. In these initial conversations, people take every word that you say to heart, and you don't want to set yourself up for failure later on. Their honest feedback will provide more insights to validate or invalidate hypotheses and help inform your eventual strategy and action plan.

In preparation for these 1:1 meetings, let your team know the questions you'd like them to answer in advance. This will give them time to mentally prepare. Don't be surprised if high achievers go a step further by preparing written documents or sharing their personal credo. Be gracious and patient because they want to set a good first impression.

As you begin to build relationships within and outside of your direct team, identify who can be part of your "wise council." Like your "board of directors" that will be discussed in chapter 4 to provide guidance on your career, the handpicked people in your wise council provide a sounding board in matters concerning the business and team. They can be internal or external to the organization and at any level—peers, direct reports, and people higher and lower in the organization. Consider a mix of attributes, including people with longer tenure who understand the historical context, functional experts, politically savvy people who understand the dynamics of the people involved, and people whose strengths are different than your own. I can't stress the last attribute enough. As human beings, it's natural to gravitate toward people whose thoughts and perspectives are like ours. However, we do ourselves a disservice by discouraging or ignoring divergent opinions. Inviting diverse thoughts and addressing them as a necessary part of achieving success can strengthen proposed ideas and initiatives and help us to be prepared for the vetting and influencing process.

MEETING CADENCES

Impromptu conversations help to keep pace with an ever-increasing speed of business. It's important to define and implement a predictable meeting cadence. For example, I schedule weekly sixty to ninety minute team meetings with my direct reports, monthly 1:1s with direct reports, monthly all-team meetings, and quarterly performance and developmental conversations with my direct reports to discuss goals, progress toward goals, and support needed, as well as a year-end review. I also host skip-level meetings with my direct reports' teams at least annually. In addition to an open-door policy and engaging individuals during monthly all-team meetings, this helps keep pulse with what's happening in the organization, their level of engagement, and how you can help them accomplish their professional goals. Depending on your communication preferences and that of your leadership, you may also want the team to send a written summary on what's happening with the business. While it adds another task on the to-do list, it also helps create a discipline of thorough communication and business mastery, especially for businesses with lots of moving parts and details.

Monthly meetings provide an opportunity for guest speakers and special topics of importance to the business, people, and organization. Inviting guest speakers from within the company provides exposure to create a more well-rounded team and breaks up the monotony of inter-team conversations. In addition to your direct team, it may be beneficial to invite key cross-functional business partners, especially for standing agenda items, which may include

- Opening comments by the leader to cover a variety of just-in-time topics.
- Recognition—an open forum for individuals to recognize each other and business accomplishments great and small. This fosters a positive outlook and team culture where people feel appreciated, and it's convenient with minimal effort required.
- Financial performance overview—share actual performance compared to budget expectations and current versus prior year. This is an opportunity for employees to demonstrate their command of the business and to identify if interventions need to be made to realize the performance targets.

- Roundtable—an open forum for team members to share what they've been working on, key learnings, accomplishments, and barriers.
- Icebreaker—ask a lighthearted question to continue team bonding by focusing on the team as people, not just employees. Asking questions that are too serious can put undue pressure on your team and bring the spirit of the meeting down. Be thoughtful about the diverse composition of your team to avoid unintentionally offending anyone.

Lighthearted Icebreaker Questions

1. If you could vacation anywhere in the world, where would it be?
2. Who would you most like to be stranded on an island with?
3. What's your favorite dessert?
4. If you won the lottery, what would you do?
5. If you could have front row seats to any concert, who would you see?
6. If you could have an endless supply of any food or drink, what would it be?
7. Who would you like to trade places with for one month?
8. What's a little-known fact about you?
9. What's your favorite charity?
10. What is your favorite cartoon character?
11. What was your favorite TV show growing up?
12. What's your favorite TV show network?
13. If your life was made into a movie, who would play you?
14. What's your most used emoji?
15. What's your favorite cell phone app?
16. What's your favorite sport?
17. If you had a superpower, what would it be?
18. If you weren't working in your current profession, what career would you do instead?
19. If you had to sing karaoke, what song would you pick?
20. If you didn't have to work to earn a living, how would you spend your time?
21. If you had a personal assistant, what would you have them do?

22. If you could instantly be an expert in a subject, what would it be?
23. What is one of your biggest pet peeves?
24. If you had a time machine, would you go back in time or into the future?
25. If you had your own late-night talk show, who would you invite as your first guest?
26. Imagine you're a featured speaker for a huge event. As you're walking onto the main stage, what's your entrance music?
27. If you could have dinner with any famous person from any point in history, who would it be?
28. Describe yourself using only three words.
29. What's the most memorable vacation you ever took?
30. Which season fits your personality best—spring, summer, fall, or winter—and why?

NINETY DAYS IN

After you've been on the job for ninety days, it's an opportune time to reflect on all that you've learned, key observations, and early wins. Capture this information to share with your manager as a head start to your performance review. Completing this template every ninety days helps to realize your accomplishments and shape your personal brand. A simple template is shown in figure 3.1.

The first ninety days is like a honeymoon period. As time passes, you become more comfortable in your role with your new team and vice versa. About four months after starting a new role as a leader, it's a great opportunity to conduct a new leader assimilation workshop. Typically hosted by your human resources (HR) business partner, this session is an opportunity for your direct team to deepen their relationship with, and understanding of, you in a confidential, nonthreatening way. It also provides you feedback and a pulse check on how things are going in your new role with this key constituency.

Here's how a new leader assimilation works.

Step 1:   Block the date for a four-hour session, preferably at an off-site location and including a meal. Schedule the session at a time when everyone from your team, as well as the facilitator, is available.

First 90 Days – Your Name Here

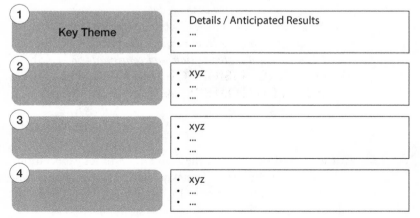

Next 90 Days – Your Name Here

Figure 3.1.   **First 90 Days Next 90 Days**

Step 2:   Send out an email to set expectations for the session. The following would be one example:

> *Dear Team,*
>
> *It's hard to believe that we're wrapping up the first three
> months as a new team. As we continue to work together, I've
> asked* [INSERT NAME OF FACILITATOR] *from our HR
> team* [OR OTHER FUNCTION] *to facilitate a new leader
> assimilation workshop. This is a process where, as a team, you can
> ask questions about me, my operating style, priorities, and offer me
> advice on how we can be successful together.*
>
> *The meeting is planned for* [INSERT DATE] *from*
> [START TIME to ENDING TIME]. *Your attendance is
> critical to the success of the process.*
>
> [FACILITATOR] *will facilitate and record the discussion
> around the questions below without me present.*
>
> *1. What do you value/appreciate about* [LEADER]*?*
> *2. What don't you know about but would like to know about*
> [LEADER]*?*
> *3. To increase effectiveness, what should this* [LEADER] *start,*
> *stop, or continue?*
>
> *Once you have an opportunity to answer the questions,* [FA-
> CILITATOR] *will debrief me and then I'll return to the session
> and we can go through my answers/responses as a team.*
>
> *Here are a few ground rules for the session.*
> * *Nothing you say is attributable—I won't know who says what.*
> * *There are no sacred cows—everything is on the table.*
> * *Confidentiality among team members is critical.*
>
> *I look forward to the session and continuing to* [INSERT
> MOTIVATING VISION OF WHAT YOUR TEAM
> DOES FOR CUSTOMERS] *led by this amazing team.*
>
>   *Sincerely,*
>   [YOUR NAME]

Step 3:   At the start of the session, the facilitator will set expectations,
including an invitation of honesty and confidentiality among
the team as well as vulnerability from the leader. He or she
will also preview the remaining steps in the process.

Step 4:   The new leader can provide a brief biographical sketch. Although this may have already been done at the Day 1 meeting,
time has passed and sharing again could serve as a refresher
or take on new meaning. The team is free to ask follow-up
questions in the relationship-building process.

Step 5:   The facilitator asks the new leader to exit the room while they
conduct the session as outlined in the premeeting email. This
can take one to two hours.

Step 6:   After the facilitator asks the questions above and captures the
feedback on a flip chart, they dismiss the team and have a conversation with the leader to brief them on the feedback themes
and questions they will be asked to answer when the full team
comes back into the room. None of the individual identities of
people who asked questions or provided feedback are revealed
overtly or through use of language that would easily identify
the source. This preview session, normally twenty to thirty
minutes in length, gives the leader an opportunity to mentally
and emotionally prepare for a moment when the strength of
their leadership will be on full display.

Step 7:   The team is invited back into the room and the facilitator goes
through each of the questions, providing greater context for
the conversation that was had when the leader was out of the
room. The leader will also answer questions and respond to
the feedback themes the team members shared.

To say that this is a vulnerable experience is an understatement.
Since it's difficult to fully predict what's in the minds and hearts of other
people, and candor is encouraged in this exercise, you never know what
someone will say or how they will feel. The questions people want to
know about can range the gamut, from opinions on specific topics to
political affiliation to reflection questions like the biggest mistake you've
made in your career.

This exercise also leverages all four emotional intelligence domains, including self-awareness of your emotions as you listen to the
feedback, self-management—responding with very little preparation
time to questions of all sorts, and organizational awareness when you
listen to feedback shared on how you're valued and what the team
believes you or they should change. The exercise helps strengthen the

relationships between the leader and the organization, for it is a key moment to demonstrate inspirational leadership that will help build teamwork, enable more effective coaching and mentoring, and more.

Another benefit, or risk, of your HR business partner serving as facilitator is that they hear the raw feedback from your team. As you can imagine, sometimes the feedback affirms our desired brand, and other times the feedback is constructive, pointing out opportunities for adjustment with the leader and/or team. It's in your best interest to partner with this person from HR as a member of your "wise council" during and after the session so you can develop and progress together against your personal development plan. This will help to build and shape your brand reputation, which comes in handy when talent review season comes around.

THE NEXT NINETY DAYS AND BEYOND

After you've listened and learned in the first ninety days, it's now time to develop and crystallize your vision, objectives, strategies, goals, measures, and action plan. Review the pages of notes you've taken over the past several weeks. Reflect on what changes could make the biggest differences in the outcomes, performance, and culture of the business and team. Solicit feedback from your direct reports, wise council, critical cross-functional team members, and manager.

Once you're aligned, cascade the vision and goals through all levels within your organization and cross-functional teams, as necessary. Driving clarity in the vision and goals form the building blocks that you and the team will ultimately be measured against. One tool to consider is an OGSM—objectives, goals, strategies, and measures. A template is shown in figure 3.2. This one to two page document captures the vision, strategy, and action plan in a single document that should link directly to performance goals of individuals. Be cautious about change fatigue. Changing too much at once could overwhelm your team, dilute the impact, and put them on the defense if not done thoughtfully.

Of utmost importance to any organization is the caliber of its talent. Talent management is one of the most important competencies of an effective leader. Without people, the organization will cease to exist. However, a leader needs more than warm bodies on the team. Based on the direction you're taking the business, you'll need to determine if

FY## OGSM - [INSERT BUSINESS UNIT / TEAM NAME]		Last Updated xx/xx/xx
VISION: ______		
OBJECTIVE	**GOALS**	
To ....(insert clear, concise statement)	1. GOAL #1: short explanation (i.e. revenue, profit, capabilities, talent) 2. GOAL #2: short explanation 3. GOAL #3: short explanation	
STRATEGIES	**MEASURES**	**LEAD**
Where to Play (WHO)		
1. **INSERT WHERE TO PLAY #1.** (i.e. Target audience, customers, channels, products, sales team)		
- Insert Where to play sub-strategy, project, tactic	- Insert quantifiable measure, by when	Name
-	-	
-	-	
2. **INSERT WHERE TO PLAY #2.** (i.e. Target audience, customers, channels, products, sales team)		
-	-	
-	-	
-	-	
3. **INSERT WHERE TO PLAY #3.** (i.e. Target audience, customers, channels, products, sales team)		
-	-	
-	-	
How to Win (WHAT/HOW)		
1. **INSERT HOW TO WIN #1.** (i.e. positioning, claims, points of parity/difference, competitive reference, new product/service, marketing & communications tactics, capabilities, processes, talent)		
- Insert How to Win sub-strategy, project, tactic		
-		
-		
2. **INSERT HOW TO WIN #2.** (i.e. positioning, claims, points of parity/difference, competitive reference, new product/service, marketing & communications tactics, capabilities, processes, talent)		
- Insert How to Win sub-strategy, project, tactic		
-		
-		
3. **INSERT HOW TO WIN #3.** (i.e. positioning, claims, points of parity/difference, competitive reference, new product/service, marketing & communications tactics, capabilities, processes, talent)		
- Insert How to Win sub-strategy, project, tactic		
-		
-		
4. **INSERT HOW TO WIN #4.** (i.e. positioning, claims, points of parity/difference, competitive reference, new product/service, marketing & communications tactics, capabilities, processes, talent)		
- Insert How to Win sub-strategy, project, tactic		
-		
-		

Figure 3.2. OGSM Template

- The right talent is in place, with the necessary experience to deliver goals and objectives.
- The right talent is on the team, but they lack the skills, experiences, and/or are unwilling or unable to close learning gaps necessary to deliver goals and objectives.
- The right talent is on the team but with the wrong roles and responsibilities.
- The talent is valued and better suited for other areas of the business outside of your team or with other functions across the organization.
- The talent isn't a good fit for the organization.

Your assessment of the team will determine your path forward, whether it's to nurture and develop high-performing talent, close skills gaps, provide mentoring and coaching, or to coach employees out of the team or organization. Partner with your manager and HR business partner on your observations, strategies, and plans to solicit support and enable the most success executing your talent strategy.

These strategies and tools will put you on a fast start to building credibility and relationships in your new role and with a new team.

EMOTIONAL INTELLIGENCE INSIGHTS

16. Leadership is about learning as well as unlearning.
Every new role, team, level, and manager requires slightly different skill sets and behaviors to be successful. For example, success for an individual contributor may include productivity, accuracy, and efficiency, while success as a people leader is less about self and more about building others' capabilities.

> *"Characteristics that made you successful in your last role may not serve you well in a new circumstance."*

Once you understand what's required to be successful, act with intention to achieve better outcomes.

17. Call people by name.
The sweetest sound to a person's ear is their name . . . pronounced correctly.

> *"If you want to endear people to you as a leader, get to know them as individuals and call them by name."*

Understand their dreams and desires. Ask about their upbringing. Learn how they spend their time when they're not working. Be genuinely curious about not just what they can produce for the organization but about the person they are. When you call someone by name and have conversations beyond the task at hand, it sends a message that people matter.

18. Culture reigns supreme.

> *"Creating a culture of trust, open communication, accountability, recognition, and commitment to a common vision is the number one job of a leader."*

Without talented employees who are engaged and committed, strategies and plans are useless. Culture is shaped through language, communication, and modeling the behavior you want to see in others. Spend time in formal and informal team settings, small groups, and one-on-one engaging in two-way dialogue that motivates others, builds team spirit and identity, and brings out the best in others.

19. Clarity and accountability drive results.
Establishing a clear, compelling vision co-developed with the team drives ownership and buy-in. Breaking down the vision into strategies, goals, and owners drives accountability. Measuring progress every one to three months, including making the necessary adjustments to overcome barriers, leads to results and recognition that the individual and the team can be proud of.

"What gets measured gets done. What gets rewarded gets remembered."

20. Consider the trade-offs.
Impulsive, uninformed decision making is dangerous, especially the higher up you go in an organization.

"In business, there aren't right or wrong answers . . . only trade-offs."

Therefore, leaders should socialize ideas and seek feedback on the pros, cons, and alternatives from several stakeholders before making critical decisions. Think and feel from different people's perspectives. Then you'll feel more confident making decisions that others helped to inform.

21. Be patient for growth.

"Personal growth is a slow process."

Experienced leaders can recognize trends, foreshadow outcomes, and quickly draw conclusions. While it's tempting to feel agitated and impatient, when time permits, bring your valued employees along the journey toward personal growth. Engage in rich dialogue by sharing your observations of their actions, behaviors, and impact on others. When they understand and take personal ownership of their areas of opportunity, they're much more likely to make a positive change.

22. Hire for character, not just competence.
Hiring someone with strong competencies and experience is critical but insufficient. More important than skills are their character, values, and coachability. Can you trust them? Have you established a rapport? Do they demonstrate emotional intelligence and respond appropriately to nonverbal cues? Do they exhibit good judgment? Regardless of how well-educated people are, we learn most on the job. If the candidate is coachable, you can teach them the core skills.

"Character cannot be taught."

Hiring great talent is both an art and a science. Here are some strategies to assess these factors during an interview process:

- Have lunch or dinner with the candidate.
- Check character references.
- Invite both peers and next-level employees to join the interview panel, then listen to their feedback.
- Most of all, trust your instinct.

23. Give your employees plenty of airtime.
The higher you go, the less you know. It's not an assault on your intelligence or capabilities. If you're focused on the right priorities—talent, culture, strategy, action plans, and capabilities—you won't have the capacity or the desire to be the expert in the nitty-gritty details.

When you ask your employees for their recommendation, it sends a clear message that you value their perspective and believe in their capabilities. Allowing your employees to be the experts has many benefits:

- You build their self-esteem and self-worth.
- Since they're closest to the work and have the deepest understanding, they can share insights that may not be obvious from afar.
- You have the benefit of listening, learning, and bringing a different lens to the conversation.
- When they shine, it's a positive reflection on your leadership and investment in their development.

"Give up the desire for control.
Let your employees be the experts so you don't have to."

24. Slow to hire, swift to fire.

When team members aren't performing up to par, work swiftly toward corrective action. While it creates more work for managers, ignoring the issue only makes matters worse for the employee and the team. Worse yet, passing along a "problem" to another department does a disservice to the organization.

To start the corrective action process, ask open-ended questions about how things are going to gauge the employee's self-awareness. Create an action plan with deliverables, metrics, dates the employee can achieve, and ensure that the metrics are consistent with the expectations of the job. Have consistent, two-way dialogue about their progress at least bi-weekly, and be genuine in your desire to see them succeed.

"Regardless of the outcome of performance improvement plans, keep your employee's dignity at the forefront."

• 4 •

Using Emotional Intelligence to Influence People and Organizations

$\mathcal{A}$dvancing your career isn't a meritocracy where the best performer wins. Solid performance is critically important, especially in the early stages of your career at a new company or when you have new leadership. However, after you've proven yourself to be a consistently strong performer, over time, the role performance plays in your upward trajectory diminishes. If performance isn't enough to advance your career, then what else is required?

Early in my career, I learned about the PIE model—performance, image, and exposure. As performance becomes a baseline expectation, your image (or personal brand) and visibility (or exposure) become increasingly important as they impact your influence and advancement. Let's discuss these attributes further.

In chapter 1—"Why Great Performance Isn't Enough"—you read the step-by-step process to define your personal brand. The following thought-provoking questions illustrate how your brand is a leading indicator of your level of influence.

- What do people say about you when you're not in the room? These are the blind spots we talked about in chapter 1.
- You've already proven that you can get the job done, but are you trustworthy and credible?
- Do you engage others as an inspirational leader, or are you more reserved and task-oriented?
- Do people feel comfortable around you, or does awkwardness exist?

- Have you adapted to the company and organizational norms, or are you seen as a square peg trying to fit into a round hole?

This is not to say that you need to be a clone to succeed or that you need to be best friends with everyone. We are each fearfully and wonderfully made with unique skills, perspectives, and experiences. However, if you're off-putting or rub people the wrong way, chances are that your brand reputation could be a barrier to your career advancement in your present company or organization. When you're a consistent performer who is liked, then you can be trusted. In most cases, once you are trusted, then you will be considered for expanded and elevated roles.

The E in PIE stands for exposure. No man or woman is an island. Since it's impossible to lead if you have no followers, it's also impossible to influence without forming strategic, mutually beneficial relationships. This requires a diverse network. There are many groups where you can gain exposure to grow your influence: manager, peers, direct reports, your network, your board of directors, and yourself. Let's discuss each stakeholder in greater detail.

MANAGING UP: MANAGERS/LEADERS

Your manager should be one of your biggest advocates among their peers and superiors. Since they are most familiar with your performance when you are "managing up," a good manager also gathers feedback from not only their peers, but also from your peers and direct reports. The combination of their personal experiences and broad-based feedback forms their perception of you. Without your manager's support, getting promoted is a difficult feat.

MANAGING DOWN: DIRECT REPORTS

Many times, we spend more time with direct reports than with any other stakeholders. Like a marriage, they see us at our best, and they see us at our worst. Unlike managers and senior leaders who generally engage in meetings where we benefit from significant preparation and are generally more polished in our delivery and intentional in our communication, we interact with direct reports and other team members in more informal settings. They get to see the "real you," which is the true indication of character.

Your team is the first litmus test of leadership because without followers, there is no leader. Just because you're a manager doesn't mean that you're a leader. However, being in a position of authority creates a power dynamic that must be actively managed. Titles, positions, and hierarchy create a certain deference among employees whose very careers may be at the mercy of these leaders. Managers have more say-so in decisions than employees do, even exercising veto power at times. Therefore, if you want to become a beloved influential leader, it's important to take intentional steps to neutralize these natural human behaviors that can work to your detriment if left unattended. Sometimes employees will do just enough to get by. However, if you want your team to go the extra mile, you must build followership as an inspirational leader.

MANAGING ACROSS: PEERS

Peers are an interesting stakeholder group. Peers spend a great deal of time with you but are not required to comply or agree with your directives and point of view. Because of this power dynamic, this is the most difficult yet one of the most critical stakeholder groups to influence. Think about how many functions are interdependent within your organization—sales, marketing, finance, human resources, research and development, operations, and the list goes on. Without the advocacy of cross-functional peers, initiatives can stall or die altogether. On the other hand, strong engagement leads to advocacy, which builds momentum and greater success.

Let me share a couple personal stories about the importance of peers. When I started my career in a global, functionally interdependent Fortune 500 company, I soon came to realize that one of my weaknesses was being averse to criticism. I take great pride in my visions and work contributions, and while I wasn't quite a know-it-all, I felt that my work was just shy of a masterpiece. OK, that's a little over the top, but hopefully you get the picture.

This company I worked for is known for its one-page memos. Regardless of how long you've worked on a project, in order to communicate the initiative up the ranks, you need to synthesize it into a one-page, single-spaced memo with no less than 10-point font. I had a trial by fire the summer I interned. My one-page memo had no less than six rounds of edits—in red pen. I felt small and unintelligent, as if my competence had been questioned. I resolved to work even harder to be more diligent in the front end and avoid so many rounds of edits on the back end.

That summer, I received an offer and returned two years later when I finished my undergraduate and MBA programs. I worked on a cross-functional initiative with a different manager and was determined to apply what I learned during my internship. However, in hindsight, when it came time for feedback I was more focused on selling my seemingly brilliant idea than collaborating to create an even better one. Analyzing my thoughts and feelings, I had convinced myself that my way was the best and maybe the only way. Thank goodness for a manager who helped me see the light, as illustrated in figure 4.1.

"Kristin, do you see this perfect circle?" he asked as he drew on the whiteboard in his office. "It represents what seems like your perfect idea" *(Figure 1)*. "When other people provide feedback, it starts to put dents in your perfect circle" *(Figure 2)*. What he said made sense to me. I felt that feedback from others was criticism of the idea—and of me. I was annoyed because others found fault in my idea, even after all my hard work in developing what I thought was a compelling business case. Those "dents" represented unwelcome feedback and blemishes to my "perfect" idea.

He went on to say, "The benefit of collaboration is creating a new idea together. This new creation turns out better than the original because it leads to more buy-in. People feel heard. And it transforms from *your* perfect idea to *our* idea" *(Figure 3)*.

Several light bulbs clicked in my head, and I still remember these valuable lessons nearly twenty years later and how they illustrate emotional intelligence:

- No man or woman is an island, in life or work. Therefore, very little is accomplished single-handedly. *(EI competency: teamwork)*

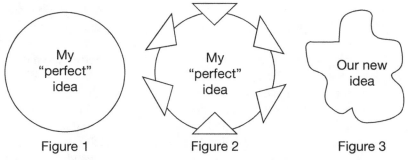

Figure 1   Figure 2   Figure 3

Figure 4.1.   Ideas

- The more buy-in you have, the greater the odds of success. *(EI competency: conflict management)*
- Gathering feedback strengthens the odds of success for an idea, project, or work product by asking questions, making suggestions, scenario planning, and identifying potential roadblocks. *(EI competency: achievement orientation)*
- No matter how smart or accomplished you are, you're doing a disservice to the organization and team if you don't leverage other people's knowledge, skills, and experiences. Their feedback wasn't an assault on my intelligence—it was an opportunity to build a coalition of allies. Contributions from other people—whether subject matter experts, generalists, the end users, or other stakeholders—are just as important as your own. *(EI competencies: empathy, organizational awareness)*
- If you give up "pride of ownership," the result of what you create together will often be much better than how it started on your own. *(EI competencies: adaptability, positive outlook)*

It was a humbling experience that led to my growth and continued development. Many years later, I had another "aha!" moment around peer relationships. The results of a 360 showed that leadership had a very high opinion of me, as did direct reports. However, among peers, I had work to do. As I worked with my executive coach to deconstruct the situation, she helped me realize that the impact of being an only child whose extracurricular activities focused on individual pursuits, such as playing the piano and serving in leadership roles, had trickled into my work life. How would a seemingly unrelated demographic fact impact my work performance, you might ask? It showed up in conflict management.

My parents raised me to be an independent go-getter. My father was a salesman and my mother was a social worker by trade who sold so much crystal at home parties that it became her full-time job. I grew up handwriting crystal party invitations, affixing labels and stamps to envelopes, and even conducting some of the parties as young as ten years old when my mom was double-booked with other parties.

I had been blessed with creative visions and new ideas from a young age. One Christmas I wanted to buy presents for my family and friends but didn't have any money. I was only thirteen years old. During a routine thirty-minute walk to school, I got the bright idea to sell baked goods to earn money for Christmas gifts. That vision turned into "Krissy's Cookies 'n' Stuff," a baking endeavor that led to $100 profit that Christmas. I continued baking for family, friends, and church members until I graduated high school.

There's nothing like the feeling of accomplishing what you've envisioned and worked so hard to achieve. From church organizations to high school to student government in college and beyond, I have always enjoyed leading people. I've typically served as president, vice president, or chairperson, as I have a gift for administration. While these leadership roles don't give unilateral authority, they each carry weight that has more influence than, let's say, a committee member or volunteer. When conflict arose, since I was often the leader, I would usually have the final say.

The experiences as an only child and student leader in my formative years led to much more influence than the corporate environment could offer, where I now must influence peers with whom I have no authority or reporting relationships. Even though marketing, my functional expertise, has often been the core decision-making function with profit and loss responsibility, I've learned that my position and title are not the only levers that can be pulled to influence others. Further, in the past when conflict arose, my default behavior was to escalate the situation to my boss or another leader higher in the organization. To my peers, this was the equivalent of being a tattletale.

As an only child, I've never experienced sibling rivalry. I haven't had to collaborate with siblings to persuade Mom and Dad as a united force, nor have I negotiated with siblings to solve problems before our parents found out about our misbehavior and we got in more trouble. Instead, as an only child, my frame of reference was to "power through it" and escalate when necessary. In hindsight, although I rarely share an observation without also sharing a recommended solution or course of action, I often felt like I was just complaining. Moreover, my peers felt betrayed, and escalating the situation often put leaders in an awkward, no-win position.

With heightened self-awareness and empathy, I was determined to win over peers and turn them into personal enthusiasts. So I adopted a new approach and created a "wise council" with whom I could consult, usually in one-on-one settings, to gather input and feedback. Peer leadership is critical and unconstrained by reporting structure. Even if their roles and responsibilities aren't related to the project or idea, soliciting their opinions and tapping into their expertise makes them feel valued. This dialogue creates a mutual exchange that is invaluable the higher up you go in an organization. Strategic, intentional engagement that included peers neutralized my critics and strengthened the resolve of my supporters. Engagement should be a critical part of every leader's strategy.

MANAGING BEYOND: YOUR NETWORK

It has been said that your network equals your net worth. While this phrase applies to your income potential, it also impacts your influence. However, networking can be a daunting task for several reasons:

- We first need to gain access to our target audience, which can sometimes pose barriers.
- It takes courage to strike up a conversation with someone you don't know well, especially for people with introverted personalities.
- Without chemistry and/or some mutual connection between two parties, networking can feel awkward.
- Networking doesn't typically have immediate benefits; it takes patience to build and nurture a relationship over time.
- If there is something you want to gain from the other person, it requires a thoughtful approach so they can see the mutual benefits of what you're requesting.

- It's fraught with risk and the potential for disappointment and rejection.

Throughout my career, I've been paired with mentors and have also sought out people to network with, often leaders in more senior positions. I've experienced every one of the bullet points above, especially when I've initiated a networking relationship based on someone's title or position. The meetings were generally awkward, and it rarely yielded benefits for either of us.

On the other hand, I've also experienced many fruitful networking relationships. Networking, if approached authentically, thoughtfully, and with no fixed end in mind, can yield immeasurable benefits. Think of it as an archeological dig—you're on a journey to see what you can discover. There are few to no expectations and, therefore, less room for disappointment. Networking with hopeful anticipation, yet a balance of ease and grace, will feel more comfortable for you and the other party. Some of the strongest networking relationships have been birthed out of introductions from mutual colleagues or friends and from interacting in situations where there is a mutual interest, such as a project, team, community board, or organizational affiliation. It's also beneficial to have networks with diverse experiences, perspectives, and acumen. If you're the smartest person in your circle, you need to find a new circle.

To advance your agenda, there are times when you need to strategically engage other people for information, feedback, access, buy-in, or approval. There's nothing wrong with establishing short-term alliances. As they say in politics, "no permanent friends, no permanent enemies." These alliances are transactional and short-term in nature because they're focused on accomplishing a specific task, for a specific benefit, in a specific timeframe. Networking is different. The key to networking is to build goodwill before you have a need. It takes time and effort, but the benefits of engaging and developing relationships with a broad group of people far outweigh the comforts of keeping a very tight circle of acquaintances.

When networking in the workplace, there are three types of approaches I often see: (1) setting up time to meet face-to-face, (2) strategic communication, and (3) just-in-time communication. Without building a strong foundation in person and nurturing the relationship based on what's important to the other person, just-in-time communication becomes more transactional and less strategic. So it's important to build rapport. Let's talk about each of these in more detail.

Face-to-Face

Rapport is most quickly built through in-person dialogue. I used to bring specific agendas, sometimes even typed, to networking conversations. Reflecting on this approach, I broke all the unspoken rules because I was imposing my priorities on the other party. It felt forceful and one-sided. I may have accomplished what I set out to learn or do, but it left the other person feeling used. That isn't to say that you should walk into a conversation without aim or predetermined thoughts. The point is to give up a fixed agenda and, instead, go with the flow. Now, I write short bullet points in my journal to remind me of the topics I want to cover. While I may glance at them during the conversation, I let the conversation take its natural course. Taking a lighthearted, informal, or unstructured approach leaves both parties feeling more comfortable.

Strategic Communication

If you help people get what they want, they're more likely to help you get what you want. This time-tested principle works. As you build rapport, it's critical to listen to the needs and desires of the other person and then do what you can to meet those needs. If you're not attuned to their needs and desires, what could be a strategic networking relationship will diminish into a short-term transaction.

There are several ways to nurture relationships with strategic communication:

- Check in with no other intention than to see how someone else is doing. For example, coffee chats, lunch, happy hour, or even text messages.
- Share information to keep them in the know. Within a work environment, information is one of the most valuable assets. There are countless examples of valuable information, including, but not limited to, people changes, organizational changes, category and competitive insights, news articles, and insights on

key influencers' opinions and perspectives that can advance or derail their agendas and priorities.

- Provide access to your network through formal and informal introductions.
- Give people your undivided attention, which builds their self-esteem and makes them feel valued. For example, while it's tempting to check emails on my cell phone while I'm walking around the office, choosing to make eye contact and even say hello to people I see, whether I know them or not, is an easy way to build rapport and strengthen your brand image. If it's someone I know, stopping to ask how things are going is a powerful way to informally influence others, let them know what you've been up to, and shape your personal brand. While some call it an elevator pitch, I prefer to call it strategic small talk. Always be ready.

Just-in-Time Communication

When you've built goodwill with other people, you can activate just-in-time communication, including phone calls, emails, text messages, and instant messages. Sometimes there are issues, concerns, or discussion topics that can't wait for a scheduled meeting. This informal approach creates a more natural relationship that expands access and accelerates the speed of exchange and mutual benefit.

MANAGING YOUR BOARD OF DIRECTORS

This figurative term is a collection of individuals handpicked by you to provide mentorship, advice, support, constructive feedback, and advocacy in pursuit of your career advancement. These people, who probably don't know each other, all have one thing in common—they want you to succeed personally and professionally. They should be familiar with your strengths, opportunity areas, and experiences based on their personal interactions with you and the open dialogue you exchange.

These advocates also look out for you when you're not in the room and provide insight into any gaps that may exist. For example, one time during a routine one-on-one with a mentor, she provided constructive feedback that my comments to her peer rubbed the peer the wrong way. I certainly wasn't expecting to hear that feedback, but I was very grateful nonetheless. I was even happier that I'd learned to let the conversation flow naturally without a fixed agenda; otherwise, I may not have been physically, mentally, and emotionally open to hearing and internalizing this surprising feedback.

My mentor was under no obligation to share this information but did so out of genuine care for my success and professional brand reputation. The next time I spoke with the person I had unintentionally offended, I "cleaned up" my comments. I made no mention of the conversation with my mentor. Rather, I offered a blanket apology if I said or did anything that may have been misinterpreted. This teachable moment was a great opportunity for self-awareness, empathy, and social awareness of how much words and actions can have an unintentional effect on others.

Your board members may also provide access and introductions to their own network, which is an invaluable gift. After all, word of mouth is the oldest and most powerful form of advertising. In an increasingly competitive global market, having a personal connection, even if it's a "second-hand connection," can make all the difference.

These board members can include former managers and employees, current or former cross-functional business partners, friends from other companies and industries, your spouse, your coach or confidante, and even people who are unfamiliar with the specific dynamics of your work environment. You want people who can demonstrate objectivity, all with you in mind. It's especially helpful to have board members in and outside of the company or organization you currently work for because they provide diverse, equally valuable perspective.

No matter how far you advance in your career, the role these board members play will not go away. In fact, their importance intensifies because the stakes get higher. The job gets tougher, the competition gets steeper, and relationships with others can change simply because of your title, position, and the organizational dynamics. Furthermore, the higher you go, the less feedback you receive. Recall from the PIE model that if the expectation of solid performance has already been proven, the measure of your success shifts to image and exposure. Leaders don't have time or patience to train you on the technical aspects of the job, let alone provide detailed feedback on your developmental areas.

In 2016, a McKinsey & Company and LeanIn.org study showed that women receive informal feedback less frequently than men, despite asking for it more often.[1] They also have less access to senior-level sponsors. Sponsors are leaders who choose you because of your potential and are willing to exercise their political capital to advocate for your career. A key difference when compared to a mentor is that sponsors are in positions of power; therefore, their influence can make a difference in the decisions other people make about your career progress. They also choose you, not the other way around, sometimes with your knowledge and other times without. Sponsors are often privy to information before it's broadly known and participate in conversations about you that you know nothing about.

Having truth tellers on your personal board of directors is essential. They help serve as an anchor to help keep you steady when situations get a little shaky and a sounding board who will provide sage wisdom that is given with your best interest in mind.

MANAGING SELF

Self-management is one of the four domains of emotional intelligence and consists of emotional self-control, adaptability, achievement orientation, and positive outlook. In order to forge relationships that lead to greater influence, it is critical to establish, maintain, and evolve, if necessary, our personal brand (refer to chapter 1 on branding). A solid reputation and brand image are the starting points for greater influence.

The diagram in figure 4.2 illustrates each of these stakeholders in the Influence Map. Unlike our self-selected, discretionary network and board of directors, we are required to engage with people up, down, and across the organization to accomplish specific tasks and get our job done. Specifically, those stakeholders are our manager(s), employees, and peers. However, fixed hierarchical relationships don't necessarily translate to influence. As we manage each stakeholder group, we have an opportunity to build trust, establish common ground, create goodwill, advance their priorities, and address their pain points, all of which lead to greater influence. Over time, people within our circle of influence will introduce us to other people in their networks, creating an opportunity to forge even more relationships.

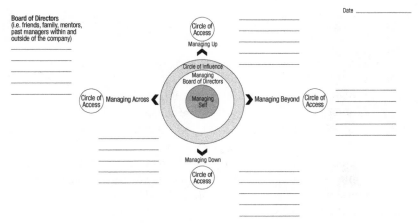

Figure 4.2.   Influence Map

Foundations of Influence

So what is influence? In essence, it's persuasion. *Merriam-Webster* offers the following definition of the verb "influence": *to affect or alter by indirect or intangible means.* An equally provocative definition is offered for the noun "influence": *the act or power of producing an effect without apparent exertion of force or direct exercise of command.*[2] In other words, influence is not a function of your title or position. Rather, influence is a subtler and more nuanced approach to changing the hearts and minds of others to get to the best decision, even when people disagree.

Here are several benefits of increasing your influence, both in general and to advance your career; you can

- Help people
- Share knowledge
- Leave a legacy
- Build self-esteem
- Deepen relationships
- Increase job security
- Expand network
- Increase income
- Achieve greater advancement

Despite these benefits, there are also common barriers and concerns around increasing influence, such as

- *Rapport*—It's easier to influence people we like and who like us in return, but it's not always necessary and shouldn't get in the way of advancing agendas that will benefit the company.
- *Commitment*—Just like trust, influence isn't instantaneous. It takes time and effort to build and nurture mutually beneficial relationships that lead to greater influence.
- *Inauthenticity*—Pretending to be someone you're not or to like someone whom you do not respect is a common barrier to increasing influence. Tapping into your self-awareness to understand and address the root cause of these feelings can lead you to feeling more peaceful and engaging in a more genuine way.
- *Conflict*—Early on in my career, I avoided any type of disagreement that could lead to conflict. As you can imagine, this didn't last long in a matrixed organization where buy-in was required from multiple functions to advance initiatives. I needed to get over this self-limiting belief and do so quickly if I wanted to perform well and advance my career. Upon reflection, I uncovered a personal belief that the only way to solve conflict was to be confrontational, an attribute I didn't respect, appreciate, or practice. However, once I challenged myself to explore other possibilities for solving conflict in a way that didn't result in bad feelings between different parties, I became more comfortable with conflict. Embrace conflict or you will handcuff your leadership potential.
- *Vulnerability*—Influence is inherently risky because you've envisioned the desired end state, but what will happen is unknown. People have their own agendas, priorities, strengths, and insecurities that may be invisible to you. Therefore, it takes courage to share your vision with others, solicit their feedback, and risk the possibility of not getting the answer you hope for. Advancing your career requires you to step out of your comfort zone.
- *Office politics*—*Webster* defines "office politics" as "the activities, attitudes, or behaviors that are used to get or keep power or an

advantage within a business or company." [3] This definition may capture the visceral reaction people have when they think of office politics because its foundation is power. While this term can have both positive and negative connotations, I contend that office politics are unavoidable, especially if you want to increase your influence.

Consider this alternate definition, from the authors of *The Influence Effect*: "We define it as the strategies and tactics that people use to gain advantage, sell their agendas, and earn support from colleagues." [4] Advancing your career requires intentional planning and action to accomplish desired outcomes. This isn't playing political games; it's being strategic. For example, let's say that you're proposing some type of change that requires alignment from other people. This is essentially selling your agenda and earning support from colleagues.

To influence other people, you must be intimately familiar with their priorities and pain points. With this insight, you'll be ready to answer the questions they're thinking:

- "Is this in line with my priorities?"
- "Does it solve a problem I face?"
- "What's in it for me?"
- "What are the risks?"
- "Are the outcomes desirable?"

Now let's address gaining advantage. Can you think of any organization that is without hierarchy? Most organizational structures are shaped like pyramids, with very few leaders at the top and more employees at each subsequent level below. If you're committed to advancing your career, you need to gain advantage against other contenders. Whether your organizational culture is highly competitive or more collaborative, make no mistake that advancing your career is a marathon with many people competing to win. As you navigate this race, consult your board of directors to find a sweet spot that is authentic to you and effective within your organization's culture.

The Process to Cultivate Influence
Plan

1. *Have an idea*—Why does this get you excited, and why should other people get on board? What's your personal conviction or motivation? What do you and the organization have to gain or lose? The content of your argument or position needs to have substance and not just sizzle.
2. *Develop a plan*—Think through the high-level details of what would need to happen to take your idea from a vision to a reality. Be careful not to be too meticulous in your planning at this stage. You want to leave enough "mental space" so there's room for other people to contribute to the idea.
3. *Develop rationale*—What's the story that will persuade people to support, act, and allocate resources? What are the benefits and potential outcomes of adopting your idea? Do you have facts to back up your reasoning? What are the benefits and drawbacks or pros and cons? What are the risks and risk mitigation plans? Consider the alternatives to demonstrate being thorough and open-minded. This may come in handy as you optimize the idea in step 6.
4. *Define stakeholder map*—Who needs to be consulted or informed? Who are the decision makers and key influencers? Who are potential allies, critics, and blockers?

Gather

5. *Solicit feedback*—The ultimate goal of influence is to get a yes; however, the more immediate task is to gain buy-in. Gathering feedback on the plan, rationale, risks, and alternatives allows you to see the situation from multiple perspectives and understand who else needs to be engaged in the conversation. Meeting in person is more beneficial than email and phone calls because you can pick up on nonverbal cues that increase your empathy, lead to greater organizational awareness, and help you understand how easy or difficult the path to yes will be. If a face-to-face meeting isn't possible, meeting by phone is an option. However, it is very difficult to influence electronically.

While it is tempting to restrict feedback providers to those who will support the idea, it's critical to engage critics to understand their issues, concerns, or fears. Listen to what they say and think a little deeper about what's not being said to truly understand what the disagreement or lack of support is about and to empathize by seeing this situation from their point of view. With supporters and critics alike, you may need to negotiate to gain approval.

Optimize

6. *Optimize idea and plan*—Based on the feedback you've gathered from diverse stakeholders, modify your idea and plans enough to align your supporters and neutralize your critics so much that adoption of the idea will be difficult to resist. This could range from slight tweaks to a major overhaul to a totally new idea or even abandoning the idea altogether. Remember to avoid pride of ownership; the goal is to transform it from *your* idea to *our* idea.

Align

7. *Align supporters*—With your revised idea and plan, have a series of 1:1 meetings with key influencers and decision makers to gather buy-in and appeal to their motivations and priorities. Seek preliminary approval for the necessary resources (i.e., people, budget, technology) to implement the idea prior to the final decision. This may consist of the same stakeholders in step 5, their managers, and/or the decision makers. This is the infamous "meeting before the meeting." While it takes more time and may turn some people off, depending on your company culture, failing to do so can lead to greater risk that your idea isn't approved or adopted.

8. *Decide*—Gather decision makers, in whatever forum is typical for your organization, to make the final decision. This often happens in meetings where multiple stakeholders gather in person and/or over the phone to solicit approval and resources

to proceed. Be prepared to review the recommendation, its benefits, risks, alternatives, resources required, and next steps.

Meetings are the primary "stage" for building or diluting influence and shaping your brand image. It's how work gets done in most office settings; therefore, it's an invaluable forum to showcase the personal brand purpose, character, value, and differentiators you developed in chapter 1. It's also an opportunity to showcase strong collaboration across levels, functions, and stakeholders. The work you've done in steps 1 through 7 will enable you to deliver a persuasive, unanimous message that is supported not just by you, but also by many others, including the direct reports of decision makers in the room. This united front increases the credibility of the idea and mitigates risk in the minds of decision makers who expect their teams' active involvement in shaping the recommendation. Influence is shaped by consistency, persistence, and unanimity.

While you may be excited to have reached this decision milestone, be dispassionate in your words and tone of voice. Too much enthusiasm, positivity, pessimism, or defensiveness diminishes trust. Instead, present a balanced point of view that engages both the head and the heart while also proactively addressing each stakeholder's interests and concerns.

You should also anticipate that people will make comments, ask questions, or seemingly "poke holes" in the plan, even when you've already aligned them in previous steps. Resist the urge to feel attacked or respond impulsively. Social influence is a powerful force, and the power dynamics are very different in group settings versus one-on-one conversations and smaller forums. Chances are that their comments are not personal. More than likely, they're managing their personal brand with the stakeholders they are personally trying to influence for reasons that may have nothing to do with you or the topic at hand.

On the other hand, sometimes there are critics whose comments can have a devastating impact on the dynamics in the room, actions and beliefs of others, and the decision itself. Someone who is willing to go against the grain could be dismissed, demeaned, ostracized, or ignored by more powerful people. Alternately, they could gain a powerful platform that raises doubts in the minds of other stakeholders and decision makers and ultimately derail your plans. If this is a new concern that you haven't already uncovered and addressed in the previous process steps, listen attentively, ask questions for clarification, commit to timely resolution, and follow up if the group isn't comfortable committing to a firm decision during the meeting. If the idea is not approved because there is more work to do, don't be discouraged. It may feel like a personal blow, but the story's not over. Manage your impulses and emotions, at least publicly. Reflect on what could have been different, learn, develop a plan of action, execute, and come back to the follow-up meeting even more prepared to secure the yes you've work so hard to hear.

Execute

9. *Implement*—Assuming you receive approval to proceed, execute the plan you laid out. Pivot when necessary if the plans and actual circumstances don't align. It's also important to provide periodic updates, whether formal or informal, to keep key stakeholders abreast of the results. This reinforces PIE by demonstrating continued performance, building your brand image, and gaining exposure with people who can play a hand in the success of your initiative, thereby advancing your career.

INSPIRATIONAL LEADERSHIP

I want to close this chapter with some thoughts on inspirational leadership. In order to lead, people must follow. While title, position, and authority will naturally enable some measure of deference, gaining influence requires proactive thoughtfulness in word, action, and conduct.

The Bible says, "Where there is no vision, the people perish" (Proverbs 29:18). Creating a vision that people can understand, rally around, and measure is the first step in influencing your organization. This leads to clarity on what the action steps are that need to be completed, by whom, and when. Identifying success metrics up front provides a goalpost to periodically measure, then celebrate, progress. The further down in the organization, the more tactical and mundane work can become. Therefore, to build followership and influence, recognition cannot be underestimated.

Below is a letter I sent to my direct team and cross-functional teams after nearly a year of preparing for a product launch. As context, we were tasked by senior leadership to meet a very aggressive goal, resulting in an extraordinary amount of effort by a very small team. This is one of my proudest and most effective moments in expanding influence.

> *One of my favorite memories as a child was taking a family vacation on an Amtrak train from Seattle to Los Angeles.*
>
> *The trip was nearly two days long, yet the time went by fast because there was so much to experience and see. From the mountains to the valleys to the oceans, I was in awe of our country's natural beauty.*
>
> *But there are some questions that have stuck with me since that tender age of fourteen. Who were the pioneers that braved unknown terrains to create a passageway for trains directly through mountains? And how did they build train tracks in between two mountains that were literally sky high, seemingly suspended in midair?*
>
> *What type of resolve did they demonstrate, and what type of mindset did they have to accomplish these seemingly impossible tasks, well before the conveniences of modern technology?*
>
> *Like these pioneers, we find ourselves in the midst of a seemingly impossible task in an unknown terrain. While we don't know what they were thinking while building those train tracks, I'm willing to assume that, like us, they ran into some stumbling blocks along the way and, at times, were discouraged. When you're building a train track a thousand feet in the air, I can only imagine how many times a bridge collapsed trying to connect the two sides.*
>
> *They weren't immune to setbacks and casualties along the way, and, yes, we've had our share of defeats as well. At times it may have seemed like there was no hope in sight, but had they given up, the millions of people who crossed that bridge would have never experienced that part of the United States of America. And many years later, those images would not have been permanently etched in my brain.*
>
> *But they did not give up, and they did not quit.*

And it's that mindset that stays focused on the goal and is undeterred by the type of setbacks that are bound to happen in any monumental task.

This team has demonstrated heroic effort to transform a dream into a reality. Less than two years ago, an idea was formed to launch a brand in a new channel. And expanding into this new territory has been far from smooth.

- *Nine months ago, who knew what these internal processes were or what so many acronyms meant?*
- *Who would have known that the addition of a new, unplanned product category would generate the most traction of any category previously in scope?*
- *There have been so many models of demand forecasts built that I've literally lost count.*
- *Photography. No photography. Photography. No photography. Photography. Who knew a decision could be so difficult?*

It takes a special type of person to brave the unknown and to do something that they've never done before.

Yet, despite these challenges, you persevered. You were resilient. You built new capabilities. You proved skeptics wrong. You built knowledge. You strengthened your muscle. You established processes that were previously nonexistent.

And as a result of our collective efforts, years from now, you can look back and know that YOU were the cornerstone of a new opportunity that will bring benefits to customers nationwide. And history will prove that this team paved the way for opportunities for our company and its employees.

Together we have traversed peaks and valleys to get to this point. And we have further to go. The potential is endless. Now is not the time to give up. History awaits because perseverance is the one constant of any significant accomplishment.

Our legacy will impact generations for years to come.

The very first shipments are due to go out this week, and indeed, we are at the top of our first mountain peak. The future is bright. Thank you for the character you've shown and all that you've done to get us this far on the journey.

The best is yet to come!

Most sincerely,
Kristin

EMOTIONAL INTELLIGENCE INSIGHTS

25. Facts tell, but stories sell.
To persuade others, first capture their imagination with a compelling vision and positive expectations about the future. Then, make the case of why the cost of inaction is worse than the pain of change. Describe your idea and its benefits, preferably supported by data, research, and trusted colleagues.

"Tell an emotionally rich story to bring the vision and possibilities to life."

Finally, solicit approval with a clear call to action.

26. Selling ideas without sharing potential downsides diminishes your credibility.
Change and innovation are fraught with risk. Most innovation fails. Sharing the potential upsides without addressing risks is telling a one-sided story.

"Build trust with influencers and decision makers
by proactively identifying and sharing risks."

Take it one step further by developing contingency plans with peers. You'll become more believable and credible in the process.

27. It's natural to be passionate about your idea, but often passion is not enough.
An idea is like a match. Instantly, it creates a light that's full of energy. When that energy inspires others, magic happens. When you're open to different perspectives, others build upon your idea to create something even better that they are personally vested in. Buy-in builds advocates, and cross-functional support helps decision makers feel more comfortable and confident.

"Without the support of other influencers, seeking approval
and resources for your ideas may be an uphill battle."

28. Incentives drive behavior.
Businesses and organizations are intentionally set up with a variety of functions that create healthy tension. For example, the goal of sales

is to satisfy customers at all cost, even if it means reducing the price, while marketers' goals are to drive demand that maximizes profit and minimizes cost.

"If you want to influence others, understand how they are rewarded and what constitutes their personal success."

Then, appeal to what motivates them.

29. Why meet before the meeting?

"The larger the group, the higher the stakes."

Some people think it's a waste of time to meet before the meeting. However, a single dissenter can instantly change the group dynamic and tone and alter the desired outcome. Meeting with key influencers prior to the team meeting allows you to learn, understand, and proactively address their concerns so the initiative doesn't stall. You can also more openly discuss and even debate privately to avoid embarrassment or tension in a larger group setting. Plus, prealignment creates advocates who might speak up on your behalf and influence their peers and leaders during the team meeting.

30. Control the "controllables."

I believe that 95 percent of life is out of our control. In many ways, people's words, actions, behaviors, and interpretations of what you say and do are uncontrollable and unpredictable. Your best intentions can be misunderstood. You can be the most favored employee one day, but in an instant, everything can change. Your manager or sponsor can leave the organization or lose their power and influence. Change is emotional. Be aware of how these uncontrollable situations make you feel. While you can't control the situation, you can control your response.

"Respond with intention instead of reacting with impulse."

31. Every organization has its own DNA.

To gauge the pulse of your organization, observe the values, norms, and culture of people.

"Pay attention to what types of behaviors are rewarded and shunned."

Combining these observations with feedback from others about your personal style equips you with powerful insights. If there's tension between your style and the organization's DNA, tweak your approach to increase effectiveness.

32. Diversify your network.
It's natural to gravitate toward people with easily identifiable similarities. It's important to dig deeper to create one-on-one connections with a more diverse network. This helps to build and maintain cooperative working relationships to enable progress. We're all human with a need to belong. Respecting and relating well to people of diverse backgrounds transcends gender, race, title, and experience.

> *"When you're good to people for goodness' sake, the relationship will feel authentic, and you'll both benefit."*

33. Be consistent.
When you interact with people in a fair and consistent way, you're more trustworthy, and your credibility skyrockets. In contrast, when you're "hot" one minute and "cold" the next, and if you're generally unpredictable, it's difficult for people to know how, or even if, to engage with you. Identify your emotions and the root cause of why these contrasting feelings are occurring. This self-awareness will help you stayed poised, even in difficult moments.

> *"Consistency breeds integrity. Integrity breeds trust. Trust leads to career advancement."*

• 5 •

Politics

Play or Get Played

*W*hile writing this book, I surveyed over a hundred friends to ask about the biggest challenge to advancing their careers. Office politics is the challenge that rose to the top of the list, especially among women. However, after more than thirty years of leadership experience, I can say unequivocally that leadership and political competence go hand in hand. If you're committed to advancing your career, it's time to get more comfortable with political aptitude.

Organizational politics is often thought of as being insincere, manipulative, narcissistic, or pursuing selfish personal interests with no regard for others or the broader organization. While this destructive approach is true in some cases, I encourage you to consider an alternative definition of politics within the workplace: *Political competence is the use of power and social networks to achieve change that benefits people and organizations.*

Every organization is a sum of its talent, comprising individuals with diverse skills, experiences, interests, incentives, and motivations. Therefore, engaging and influencing others within your social network is necessary to avoid the alternative command-and-control environment, where directives descend from the top without negotiation or input. Effectively engaging others in a way that addresses their interests increases efficiency, deepens interpersonal relationships, expedites change, and enables mutual benefit among many interested parties.

There are many reasons people dislike organizational politics. First, the word "politics" can conjure up negative feelings related to unfavorable governmental affairs. Thinking about a two-party political system sends a signal of win–lose, contentious relationships, and opposing points of view. While politicians often promise to work "across the aisle," it rarely happens because of party loyalty and the need to maintain a particular perception among voters and donors to stay in power.

Organized politics can also get messy, causing friction between different stakeholders. Issues are often complex with trade-offs no matter what decision is made. Navigating in-person social networks is also time-consuming and emotional. It requires strategy and patience to assess the landscape, understand the decision makers, and identify and then engage influencers and blockers. Other people's points of view are not always overtly shared, especially in more public settings, which is why individual relationships are so critically important. People are often more candid in one-on-one conversations than group settings if you've established a strong foundation of trust.

Empathy relies on collaboration, not competition. However, the hierarchical structures of most organizations are wired for competition, as there are more employees at the entry level and fewer employees the higher you go up in the organization, and the top tiers are reserved for only a few people. It's natural to think of peers as competition when climbing the proverbial corporate ladder. However, competing internally is not always profitable or beneficial. Those peers could one day become your manager or your direct report. In either scenario, you will be interdependent on each other for your individual and collective success. Depending on your organization's culture, competing can erode your personal brand image. It also makes it more difficult for peers and direct reports to fully engage for fear that they may get caught in the cross fires of unnecessary internal competition. Instead, compete externally to win by delivering solutions for your customers, clients, and stakeholders.

Incentives are another source of tension that lead to organizational politics. Cross-functional teams often have varying metrics that can be at odds with their peers. For example, sales and marketing are rewarded for driving revenue and profit with as many products and services as necessary to meet market demand. However, manufacturing and supply chain are incentivized to drive the most efficiency with the fewest product and service offerings. This leads to inherent tension. Practicing the E.M.P.A.T.H.Y.® techniques noted later in this chapter can help build alliances, align others to strategic initiatives, and win together as a team.

One challenging aspect of organizational politics is having to navigate what is spoken and deciphering what's left unsaid. This is where empathy can play a vital role. Empathy is a powerful tool that allows people to place themselves in others' shoes regarding what is most important to them. It's the ability to perceive what others feel, ask questions to increase understanding, process the information, and respond appropriately. Projecting our perceptions of others without engaging in dialogue can lead to mischaracterizing someone else's feelings. To build empathy, combine perception with intentional listening.

EMPATHY PLAYS A VITAL ROLE

Defining Empathy

Empathy differs from sympathy. The ancient Greek root words of sympathy are *syn*, meaning "together," and *pathos*, meaning "suffering." Therefore, sympathy is when humans have similar feelings and shared experiences. Sympathy makes it easy to identify the feelings of others because we've shared those feelings to some extent.

Unlike sympathy, personal experience is not a prerequisite for empathy. Psychologist Carl Rogers described empathy as feeling "as if" it were you, in the moment:

> Accurate empathic understanding means that the therapist is completely at home in the universe of the patient. It is a moment-to-moment sensitivity that is in the "here and now," the immediate present. It is a sensing of the client's inner world of private personal meanings "as if" it were the therapist's own but without ever losing the "as if" quality. Accurate sensitivity to the client's "being" is of primary value in the moment-to-moment encounter of therapy; it is of limited use to the individual if the therapist only arrives at this insightful and empathic understanding of the patient's experience as he drives home at night. Such a delayed empathy or insight may be of value if the therapist has a later chance to respond to the same theme, but its value would lie in formulating his empathic response to the patient's immediate living of the relationship.
>
> The ability and sensitivity required to communicate these inner meanings back to the client in a way that allows these experiences to be "his" is the other major part of accurate empathic understanding. To sense the patient's confusion, his fear, his anger, or his range as if it were a feeling you might have (but which you are not currently

having) is the essence of the perceptive aspect of accurate empathy. To communicate this perception in a language attuned to the patient that allows him more clearly to sense and formulate his confusion, his fear, his rage, or anger is the essence of the communicative aspect of accurate empathy.

At a high level of accurate empathy, the message "I am with you" is unmistakably clear so that the therapist's remarks fit with the client's mood and content. The therapist, at a high level, will indicate not only a sensitive understanding of the apparent feelings but will, by his communication, clarify and expand the patient's awareness of these feelings or experiences. The communication is not only by the use of words that the patient might well have used but also by the sensitive play of voice qualities which reflect the seriousness, the intentness, and the depth of feeling.[1]

What can we learn about empathy from the perspective of a therapist?

- The most effective empathy is experienced in the moment, not after the fact.
- Understanding the context of the commentary helps you to sense their emotions.
- Empathy requires freedom from distractions to enable complete focus on the other person and to hear what they are saying and sense how they feel as if it were you.
- Demonstrating empathy occurs in our *response* to the other person, not in our understanding alone.
- Communicating with empathy includes what is said—our choice of words—and how it's said—the voice qualities.

When we demonstrate empathy within the work environment, it can increase influence and strengthen relationships. "Empathic capacity" is the ability to perceive what others feel, process the information, and respond effectively.[2] It's the delicate balance of appreciating the feelings of others and learning how to manage our own feelings so we can be helpful. When someone is using their power and/or social network to achieve change, tap into your empathic capacity to see the world through their eyes. When we demonstrate empathy, we can navigate organizational politics from a place of power instead of victimization or defeat. This chapter will elaborate on empathy, a competency within the social awareness domain.

Benefits of Empathy

There are several key benefits of empathy, including

- Connecting more deeply with people as humans, not just as titles, roles, or functions
- Seeing people for who they are, even if it's not who you want them to be
- Finding common ground
- Inspiring curiosity instead of judgment
- Increasing credibility
- Increasing motivation and commitment, especially among direct reports
- Engaging in more effective negotiations, collaboration, and conflict resolution

Even in the most difficult circumstances, empathy can play an important role. One of the most difficult tasks of a manager is to deliver the news to a well-meaning employee who thinks they're doing well that they are not meeting expectations. Whether it leads to an immediate severance or serves as a forewarning that things aren't working out, it puts the manager in an awkward position because the conversation comes as a surprise to the employee. This type of news triggers a cycle of grief and a range of emotions. The cycle of grief includes denial, anger, depression, bargaining, and finally, acceptance. It is possible to communicate difficult news with empathy by ensuring clarity of message, using a message-appropriate tone of voice, and demonstrating genuine care and compassion for the other person's well-being.

According to Richard Boyatzis and Annie McKee, even when sharing bad news, leaders can remain effective and respected by maintaining a calm tone of voice.[3] The most effective leaders control the situation instead of letting the situation control them. They focus on what's within their span of control and manage their emotions in the process. Going a step further by offering to lend your support during the transition process helps the other person maintain their dignity while demonstrating the golden rule to "do unto others as you would have them do unto you." This builds your brand and endears others to you, even when they are being downsized, coached out of the organization, or given tough, constructive feedback.

Empathy also correlates with high performance. The Empathy Business publishes a list of the most empathetic global companies, with an emphasis on companies in the UK and United States. The index is based on an analysis of the internal culture, CEO performance, ethics, and social media presence of 170 companies on major financial indexes. According to the 2016 study, "The top 10 companies in the Global Empathy Index 2015 increased in value more than twice as much as the bottom 10, and generated 50% more earnings, defined by market capitalization. In their work with clients, they have found a correlation as high as 80% between departments with higher empathy and those with high performers."[4]

Empathy also creates an interconnectedness of thoughts and feelings, which is described as "social intelligence" by emotional intelligence pioneer Daniel Goleman. Empathic leadership can change the brain chemistry of both leader and followers. On a chemical level, neurotransmitters endorphins, dopamine, serotonin, and oxytocin promote social bonding and inspire us to trust others through openness and cooperation. On a neural level, shared brain circuits reflect the thoughts and emotions of a leader and prompt followers to literally mimic those same thoughts and emotions.[5]

There are two additional, but less familiar, types of neurons that are important to social connectedness: spindle cells and oscillators. Spindle cells were first described by anatomist Constantin von Economo and are sometimes referred to as Economo cells. These supersized neurons act as a sort of empathic autobahn; their long, thin branches extend into other neurons, revving up the transmission of thoughts and feelings in the brain. Spindle neurons are found in the anterior cingulate cortex and insula but only in humans, great apes, and other highly social creatures such as elephants, dogs, whales, and dolphins. They are active when people experience social emotions, including empathy, love, trust, guilt, and humor, and when they self-monitor emotions. As Goleman explains it, spindle cells are important to empathic leadership because they activate our "social guidance system," which helps us make "thin-slice" judgments that, within a fraction of a second, create a rapport and resonance between leaders and followers.[6]

Oscillators, located in the central nervous system, choreograph physical movement between individuals and within groups. You see their synchronized rhythms at work with skating partners who have been together for a long time and, on a more everyday level, couples who have been married for decades. Imaging studies show that the right brain hemispheres of two musicians playing in harmony are more closely coordinated than are the left and right sides of their individual brains.[7]

Studies by Valdesolo, Ouyang, and DeSteno at Northeastern University also show that by simply tapping fingers in synchrony, subjects experienced greater trust and compassion for one another.[8] "In leadership, oscillators literally establish a physical connection among groups and between leaders and followers and may account for the contagious nature of leadership. Most workers know all too well that the emotional climate at work will be based on the mood of their leaders, which is conveyed the moment they enter a room, and the presence or lack of empathy: eye contact, facial expressions, postures, tone of voice, affect, and the physiological responses these invoke."[9]

It's commonly believed that we're either born with empathy or not, and there's not much that can be done about it. Research has proven, however, that empathy can be taught. After providing empathy training to doctors at Massachusetts General Hospital, patients rated their doctors higher on empathy scales. During the training, specific interventions were made to increase perception, enhance perspectives, and improve self-regulation skills to ensure that the doctors weren't overwhelmed by the suffering of others, resulting in personal distress. Furthermore, doctors who displayed nonverbal empathic behaviors were not only rated as warmer but also more competent.[10] In other words, demonstrating empathy can result in increased effectiveness as a leader.

Here are seven strategies to increase E.M.P.A.T.H.Y.:

Expression
Manage your emotions
Presence
Acknowledge others' feelings
Tone of voice
Humanity
Your response

- *Expression* includes our facial expressions, eye contact, and responding appropriately to honor the other person and their unique experience. They say that eyes are the window to the soul. Therefore, eye contact and facial expressions are a prerequisite to expressing empathy.

Albert Mehrabian is a professor emeritus of psychology at UCLA who studied the relative importance of verbal and nonverbal messages. He concluded that there are three elements to any face-to-face conversation: (1) words, (2) tone of voice, and (3) nonverbal behavior.[11] When communicating feelings and attitude, if any of these three elements are incongruent, tonality and nonverbal cues will override the spoken word as the more trusted form of communication. Mehrabian conducted experiments dealing with communication of feelings and attitudes (i.e., like–dislike), often abbreviated as the "3 Vs"—verbal, vocal, and visual. He concluded that

- ° 7 percent of messages pertaining to feelings and attitudes are in **the words that are spoken.**
- ° 38 percent of messages pertaining to feelings and attitudes are **in the way the words are said.**
- ° 55 percent of messages pertaining to feelings and attitudes are in **facial expression.**

- *Manage your emotions.* With empathy, there are two stakeholders to consider—the other person and yourself. When we actively manage our emotions, we can consume information without responding impulsively, letting it override our thoughts, or losing self-control. Tone of voice is affected by the two nervous system controls. One operates during the fight-or-flight response with raised or shaking voice, unmasking fear and anxiety, and the other is a calm, cool, rational voice in the face of danger. The most effective leaders maintain their cool during a storm by focusing on what they can control and conveying that they are handling the situation rather than feeling derailed by it.

  Titles, hierarchical relationships, and positional authority can be self-imposed barriers to being fully expressed and empathetic toward others. It's natural to consider whether to be transparent with our feelings in the moment, especially if you're a leader or higher in the ranked organization than others in the conversation. Based on personal experience, I recommend just being human. Feel your emotions. Express your emotions. Empathy binds us together as a human race.

- *Presence* of mind and body leads to engagement and connection with the other person. To fully listen to someone else requires an inner stillness that quiets the mind, slows down breathing, and shifts the attention away from ourselves so that we become fully attentive to the other person. Physically relaxing your body, unfolding your arms, grounding yourself through deep breathing, and leaning in helps to be fully present in the moment. Silencing and putting away cell phones and electronic devices helps to limit and avoid distractions that disrupt you physically and emotionally. Being fully present and free from distractions helps accelerate empathy and experience emotions both as the listener and from the perspective of the other person.

- *Acknowledge others' feelings*, which is the essence of social awareness and empathy. Each person's level of emotional self-awareness and willingness to be transparent varies; therefore, true feelings aren't always overtly expressed. Engaging our imagination and asking thoughtful questions to learn, understand, and empathize improves empathic understanding by acknowledging and embodying the other person's situation without judgment, as if it were you. Further, complimenting facial expressions and presence with gestures such as nods, smiles, and positive "mmm hmms" and "ahh ahhs" builds trust by providing a safe space for the other person to be vulnerable. Empathy allows you to listen in a nonjudgmental way, even when the feelings of others are in direct conflict with your own.

- *Tone of voice* conveys over 38 percent of the nonverbal emotional content of what a person communicates.[12] In linguistics, prosody includes the elements of speech that go beyond the meaning of words and their phonetic pronunciation of vowels and consonants. Prosody[13] embodies nuanced communication that includes:

  ○ Intonation: the rise and fall of the voice in speaking
  ○ Tone of voice: variation in the pitch of the voice, reflective of how we feel and how we want others to feel

○ Stress: relative emphasis to certain syllables in a word or to certain words in a phrase of sentence
○ Pace: the speed at which you speak
○ Rhythm: the arrangement of spoken words alternating stressed and unstressed elements
○ Pitch: the relative highness or lowness of a tone as perceived by the ear

Empathy isn't just about what we say but how we say it.

- *Humanity.* Regardless of where someone sits on the proverbial totem pole, remember that people are human, with feelings, emotions, needs, desires, and insecurities. This includes leaders in the workplace and you too. When you put yourself in the other person's shoes, empathy increases.

  The process of understanding another person's perspective, termed "cognitive empathy," means "I understand what you feel."[14] Neuroscience proves that empathy is engaged in both the head and heart. The empathic process entails a hybrid of emotional and cognitive components that functionally intertwine to form the empathic state. It's triggered when we cognitively understand the plight of others, imagine how they feel, and then respond appropriately from the heart, even if we ourselves don't feel the exact same emotion.[15]

  Over the past several years, there have been numerous studies on the role of "shared neural networks" and their role in empathy. Tania Singer, formerly of the Max Planck Institute for Human Cognitive and Brain Sciences in Leipzig, Germany, conducted research with married couples to measure empathy.[16] The females were placed in fMRI scanners, and electrodes were attached to both the males' and females' hands. A painful shock was transmitted to the female participants through the electrodes. After the shock, the participants received a signal as their husband received a similarly painful shock to his hands. The females' brain activity was measured by the fMRI scanner throughout the process.

  The data showed that similar regions of the brain were activated whether a female received the shock directly or her husband received the shock. The difference, however, was the intensity. The brain's pain matrix was activated to a lesser degree when her husband received the shock. This demonstrates the power of the human brain to naturally share neural circuits with the brain of other people and to relate to feelings of pain and suffering. This research was the first of its kind to measure not only the emotions of the subject but also the emotions of others in the situation.

In the work environment, we, too, can share others' feelings by tapping into empathy. Politically charged situations and decisions can often feel overwhelming, frustrating, and even illogical. Unless the decision or behavior is unethical or harmful to others, by using the principles of empathy, especially engaging the imagination and the heart, it can diminish our natural impulsive urge to resist office politics and instead empower us to engage in a more productive way that yields better outcomes for all.

As leaders, our emotional state has a trickle-down effect on our teams. When our emotions aren't managed properly, it can spread like a toxic virus. On the other hand, when we actively manage our emotions, we have the power to shape a healthy culture where our teams feel safe and can thrive.

- *Your response* is the tangible reply to what you've heard, felt, and experienced. It encompasses social awareness for the other person and awareness and management of your own feelings and emotions. Your response includes what you say and what you don't say. How you respond in terms of your facial expressions, tone of voice, posture, gestures, demeanor, and choice of words has a significant impact on whether the other person feels like you've heard and understood them.

  Empathetic responses require us to distinguish between our own emotions and imagining how the other person feels. When you experience a strong emotional response and need time to appropriately respond, here are some techniques and phrases that demonstrate empathy:

  ○ Paraphrase what they've said to buy time and demonstrate that you understand the situation.
  ○ "I need to think about this for a moment."

- ◦ "How does that make you feel?"
- ◦ "I can imagine that feels . . ."
- ◦ "This makes me feel [fill in the blank]. I need some time to think about this."
- ◦ Sit in the stillness and silence, making eye contact and leaning in to express your heart without saying a word.

Empathy in the Digital Age

In 2016, millennials became the largest generation in the workforce, comprising 56 million U.S. workers, or 35 percent of the U.S. working population.[17] Ranging from 24 to 39 years old as of 2020, millennial employees have grown up with technology. *Time* magazine refers to people born in the internet era as "digital natives," as opposed to "digital immigrants," who grew up with traditional technologies such as TV, radio, and print and have adapted more recently to newer technology.

Digital natives' familiarity with technology impacts how they communicate, especially when compared to Gen Xers (ages 39–54) and baby boomers (ages 55–73). For example, among digital natives, 54 percent agree that "I prefer texting people rather than talking to them," compared with 28 percent of those born before the internet age.[18] Digital natives also switch media venues about twenty-seven times per nonworking hour—the equivalent of more than thirteen times during a standard half-hour TV show, while digital immigrants switched media venues seventeen times per nonworking hour.[19] "Young people are using media switching and swapping 'to regulate their moods,'" said Betsy Frank, chief research and insights officer at Time Inc. "They don't let themselves get too high or low if they just switch." This is an intriguing strategy to manage one's emotions.

Here are a few more statistics on digital media consumption across generations:

- Since 2000, the average American's weekly time spent on the internet has increased from 9.4 hours to 23.6 hours.[20]
- Accessing the internet from a mobile device has risen from 23 percent in 2010 to 84 percent in 2017.[21]
- Smartphone email use has increased from 21 to 79 percent, and music streaming has increased from 13 to 67 percent.[22]

- Americans check their phone on average once every twelve minutes, which is more than eighty times a day, and 31 percent feel regular anxiety at any point when separated from their phone.[23]
- Nielsen reports that adults age 18 and over in the United States spend three hours and forty-eight minutes a day on computers, tablets, and smartphones, versus four hours and forty-six minutes watching TV.[24]
- Among adults 18 years and older, 34 percent of daily time is spent on the internet or app/web, compared to 43 percent for adults 18–34.[25]

Within the workplace, the advent of technology has led to a more demanding pace of work. Cell phones have become a pervasive presence in our society and are often subtle background objects in team and one-on-one meetings alike. Mobile devices provide social connection, delivering a feel-good hormone called dopamine. Dopamine is associated with feelings of euphoria, bliss, motivation, and concentration. Released by brain cells called neurons, dopamine is a neurotransmitter that passes signals throughout the brain and to body systems and functions such as movement, sleep, learning, mood, memory, and attention. Inadequate dopamine can lead to conditions including, but not limited to, depression. Several illegal recreational drugs stimulate the release of dopamine, leading to addiction because people are always seeking pleasure through higher dopamine levels.[26] The desire to feel good can interfere with engagement and empathy.

While social media use and digital communication are nowhere close to the consequences of illegal drug use, these social connections create a craving for the next like, comment, share, direct message, or gaming win. Several studies have noted that the mere sound of an incoming notification releases more dopamine than the message content itself. Digital marketing experts estimate that most Americans are exposed to 4,000 to 10,000 advertisements each day.[27] With so much content competing for our focus, there is speculation that attention spans will be increasingly challenged and shortened.[28]

The mere presence of a cell phone is distracting and disruptive. In a series of experiments, University of Essex psychologists found that having a cell phone between two people chatting was highly distracting and disrupted the flow of other conversations.[29] Unlike cell phones, other objects like books and notebooks didn't diminish the subjects' feelings of closeness and connectedness in the same way a phone did. The proximity of cell phones may cause individuals to think of other people outside of their immediate physical social context, diverting attention away from their present, interpersonal experience face-to-face or by phone.[30]

Research has shown that the presence of cell phones interferes with human relationships, especially where people are discussing personally meaningful topics. During a ten-minute exchange between two strangers on moderately intimate, meaningful topics such as "discuss an interesting event that occurred to you over the past month" or "discuss the most meaningful events of the past year," the presence of a mobile phone resulted in a lower quality of relationships. The partners felt less close, less trust, and less empathy than those who shared a conversation without a mobile phone present. When the conversation was more casual in nature, for example, "discuss your thoughts and feelings about plastic holiday trees," even the mere presence of a mobile phone didn't impact relationship quality, trust, or empathy.[31]

Now more than ever, there is an increased reliance on emails, text messages, and instant messaging in the workplace. These valuable tools can help to expedite work, decrease response time, collaborate with multiple stakeholders, and strengthen informal relationships. However, there are downsides that can inhibit empathy and relationship building. Our grip with technology prevents us from being fully present with others. When our brains become rewired to dissociate from human experience, we lose part of our humanity, undermining our ability to create a real connection with people.

Digital communication removes nonverbal communication such as eye contact, posture, emotion, tone of voice, and reflective listening, which causes us to miss important emotional cues and reduces our ability to listen empathically. Digital communication has no tone, relying on words alone to convey messages that could be easily misunderstood. How many times has an email, text, or instant message been misinterpreted because it lacked context or was written impulsively with less than desirable thoughtfulness? Overreliance on digital communication can create a growing sense of detachment, desensitization, and emotional indifference that increases the likelihood of misunderstandings and feelings of isolation, loneliness, and powerlessness.[32]

A more effective alternative is to have a brief face-to-face or phone conversation. This accelerates understanding and enables empathy because you can detect and observe nuanced and subtle information and nonverbal cues that can only be appreciated in person—facial expressions, eye contact, tone of voice, posture, and emotion itself—and introduced back into the conversation.

A prerequisite for empathy is being fully present in the moment and limiting distractions, including, but not limited to, mobile phones. There is no greater compliment than to give someone your full attention. To truly understand what is being said, what's left unsaid, and why requires 100 percent mental, physical, and emotional engagement. Embracing empathy and the necessary use of power and people to drive beneficial change within organizations can increase our tolerance for office politics.

EMOTIONAL INTELLIGENCE INSIGHTS

34. People first, titles second.
If it weren't for getting a paycheck, many people wouldn't work. Therefore, make it a priority to understand the motivations, desires, and fears of your manager, peers, and employees as human beings *first*.

> *"When you genuinely care about people and what matters to them, you're more likely to build a trusting relationship that will lead to better productivity."*

Being attentive to these insights also enables you to adapt your plans, behaviors, and approaches to fit the situation and their self-interests.

Here are a few of my favorite conversation starters:

- How would you spend your time if you didn't have to work?
- What's your greatest accomplishment and why?
- How do you like to be recognized?
- Describe the best team you worked on, then the worst.

35. Maximize informal communication.
Our society loves email. Some might say that we've become addicted to email. Email can leave you feeling overwhelmed and overinformed. If

you want to be more in tune with people's emotions and avoid the risk of misinterpreting tone of voice, send fewer emails and opt for more informal communication.

Unlike email, instant messages and texts are efficient ways to build rapport and communicate about low-risk topics on a just-in-time basis, even during meetings.

> *"Quick conversations are more effective than email because they enable two-way dialogue and clarity."*

36. Share your weekend highlight reel.
Every Monday, be prepared to share highlights of your weekend, as long as it doesn't erode your brand image.

> *"How you spend your time helps paint a better picture of who you are and what you value."*

When people understand your character and values, it can lead to more empathetic, trusting relationships, especially if there's a mutual connection and/or appreciation for diverse backgrounds, interests, and perspectives.

37. If it doesn't fit, don't force it.

> *"Strong mentoring relationships have a common ingredient—chemistry."*

The absence of chemistry creates an awkward experience and a waste of time. Nurture authentic relationships based on personality fit or a common cause. As a mentor, be generous with your time. Listening to diverse perspectives helps you to be more in tune with the pulse of the organization and avoid the risk of being out of touch. Plus, being a mentor is often as rewarding as being a mentee.

38. You don't have all the answers.
I know you're great at what you do, but you can't be an expert at everything. Even if you're the project manager or lead, a cursory understanding doesn't translate to deep functional expertise.

> *"Rely on the expertise of others to build camaraderie, credibility, trust, and a better outcome than what could have been created in a vacuum by yourself."*

Be generous with recognition, especially when others help take a project or idea from good to great. Showing gratitude through acts of kindness goes a long way.

39. Peers aren't your competition.

Most organizations are structured like a pyramid—there are fewer roles at the top. Personal ambition and the political landscape can create feelings of competition that lead to behavior you may regret. Stay poised to reap the benefits that come from teaming up with peers. Collaborating sharpens your skills, creates a nonconfrontational environment from which to learn and solicit feedback, builds alliances, and creates a better team dynamic for managers.

"Don't burn bridges because today's peer might be tomorrow's direct report."

40. Who you marry . . . matters.

"Choosing your spouse is one of the most important decisions you'll make in your life and career."

Since marriage is a lifelong commitment, it's the ultimate test in empathy and conflict management. Our opportunity areas at work are often similar to those at home. The ideal spouse will listen, support, cheerlead, console, encourage, and provide loving, constructive feedback to you. Careers can be an unpredictable journey, so having someone in your corner who has your back and will make personal sacrifices to support your career growth is an incredible gift.

· 6 ·

Dealing with Disappointment

*E*motional resilience is the trajectory of healthy functioning after encountering a highly adverse incident.[1] Resilience is demonstrated by how well we hold ourselves through the downsides of life. It isn't about winning the battle; it's the strength to power through the storm and keep the sail steady. It is the fine balance that we develop between our emotions and the way we let them affect all aspects of our lives—at work, at home, and in our personal, professional, and social relationships.

EMOTIONAL RESILIENCE SELF-ASSESSMENT

To self-assess your emotional resilience, give yourself a rating for each statement below:

- 0 = Never
- 1 = Rarely
- 3 = Sometimes
- 5 = Often

1. I am aware of my thoughts and feelings. _____
2. I believe in my inner potential. _____
3. I am willing to adapt. _____
4. I think before reacting. _____
5. I forgive myself and others. _____
6. I have the power to overcome difficulties. _____
7. I peacefully resolve conflict with others. _____

8. I focus on finding solutions to problems. _____
9. I express my emotions in a socially acceptable way. _____
10. I acknowledge negative emotions instead of bottling them up. _____
11. I'm able to create and sustain long-term relationships. _____
12. I'm not ashamed to ask for help when I need it. _____
13. I focus on things I can control or influence. _____
14. I can handle criticism. _____
15. I am aware of my strengths and weaknesses. _____
16. I learn from failure. _____
17. I cooperate well with others. _____
18. I focus on the present and future instead of dwelling on the past. _____
19. I believe there are people who love me. _____
20. I love myself. _____

Total score _____

Interpretation

0–34 *Low emotional resilience*: You may be oversensitive to stress, overreact, and have poor coping skills when dealing with challenges. This could be a hindrance to your job performance and career advancement. Leverage the tools in this book to strengthen your resilience.

35–69 *Average emotional resilience*: Your ability to combat stress and bounce back from challenge exists, with room for improvement with new skills, training, and practice. Once you've mastered the technical skills of your job, refining your soft skills can help avoid hitting the glass ceiling so you can continue to advance. Remember, at some point in your career, raw talent and determined ambition become less important than your personal brand image, emotional management, and the ability to influence and persuade people and organizations. Read further for tips to perfect your resilience.

70–100 *High emotional resilience*: This is a healthy target for everyone. You have a well-balanced emotional reaction to, and perception of, stress. You recognize that thoughts influence actions and generally have an optimistic mindset even in the face of a challenge. This increases your level of emotional awareness with self and influence with others.

Regardless of where you scored on the self-assessment, the nature of life's unpredictable challenges presents an opportunity for continuous improvement with our level of resilience. This chapter explores the definition of resilience and why it's important and provides practical strategies to increase your resilience.

THE CASE FOR RESILIENCE

With the advances in technology and digitization, the pace of change is accelerating rapidly. We're adapting to changes that never existed before. From rigorous digitization to the 24/7 social media influence, and from the changing professions to adapting to the ways of younger generations, it is only natural to feel emotionally exhausted by the pace of change in society and the workplace.

In a study conducted by IBM Institute for Business Value in late 2015, a survey of 5,247 business executives from twenty-one industries in over seventy countries reported that "the 'scope, scale, and speed' of their businesses were increasing at an accelerated rate, especially as the competitive landscape becomes increasingly disrupted by technology and radically different business models."[2] Change inevitably leads to stress.

A survey of over 100,000 employees across Asia, Europe, Africa, North America, and South America found that employee depression, stress, and anxiety accounted for 82.6 percent of all emotional health cases in Employee Assistance Programs in 2014, up from 55.2 percent in 2012.[3] Also, a recent large-scale, longitudinal survey of over 1.5 million employees in 4,500 companies across 185 countries conducted as part of the Global Corporate Challenge found that approximately 75 percent of the workforce experienced moderate to high stress levels—specifically, 36 percent of employees reported feeling highly or extremely stressed at work, with 39 percent more reporting moderate levels of workplace stress. The current and rising levels of stress in the workplace should be cause for concern, as there is a direct and adverse relationship between negative stress, wellness, and productivity.[4]

Furthermore, the Global Corporate Challenge study of over 1.5 million employees globally over a twelve-year period found, for example, that while 63 percent of extremely stressed employees reported above-average productivity, this number rises significantly to 87 percent among those who say they are not at all stressed.[5] In the same study, 77 percent of extremely stressed employees also reported above-average levels of fatigue and early warning signs of longer-term burnout. Burnout is a lagging indicator of chronic stress.[6]

Change is often uninvited and many times unanticipated. Therefore, it naturally evokes emotions and tests a person's ability to survive and thrive despite the change. In times of change and hardship, some people snap, and others snap back. Resilience is the elasticity people find within to recover quickly from difficulties and spring back from adversity. Deriving from the Latin word *resilio*, which means "to bounce back" or "retaliate," resilience is the "capacity to maintain competent functioning in the face of major life stressors."[7]

Time and chance happen to us all. There will be many disappointments in life and the workplace, including reorganizations, restructuring, changes in roles and responsibilities, personnel changes, broken loyalties, budget reductions, layoffs, mergers, acquisitions, downsizing, challenging feedback, relocation, and more. A person's level of resilience will determine who succeeds and who fails.

Every one of us must play the cards we've been dealt. We might desire a career life without change, adversity, or even pain and suffering, but that's asking the impossible. Since most of life is out of our control, we have to learn how to control our mindset and the corresponding response. When circumstances, challenges, and conflicts occur, we have a powerful choice to react or respond. See figure 6.1.

Reacting with impulsiveness increases the likelihood of saying, doing, or behaving in a way that you regret. It makes you feel out of control and can erode your brand image. However, choosing to respond instead of reacting and using emotional intelligence can help you to respond in a more thoughtful way that demonstrates control of your actions, attitude, and approach. The Center of Creative Leadership found that about a third of senior executives derail or plateau at some point, most often due to an emotional deficit such as the inability to build a team or regulate their own emotions in times of stress.[8] Our careers are a constant journey to navigate peaks and valleys of change, stress, and unknown territory. How we respond makes all the difference.

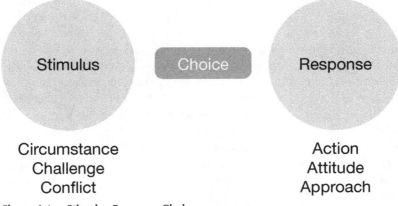

Figure 6.1.   Stimulus Response Choice

In *Work Without Stress: Building a Resilient Mindset for Lasting Success,* the authors distinguish between the definitions of pressure and stress.[9] They define pressure as a "demand to perform." The demand might be intense, but there is no stress inherent in it. The key to resilience is not to turn pressure into stress. On the other hand, when you combine pressure and rumination, it leads to stress. Rumination involves continuing to churn over emotional upsets, which prolongs the emotional discomfort, can lead to damaging effects, and results in chronic stress. Rumination isn't a by-product of stress. It *is* stress. According to the authors, if there's no rumination, there's no stress.

Emotional intelligence is a critical skill of resilient people. It involves a multilevel process—the ability to monitor the feelings of yourself and others, to discriminate between them, and to use that information when you act. Though the level of emotional intelligence varies from person to person, we all use it when coping with negative circumstances. Researchers have shown that highly resilient people tend to utilize more emotionally intelligent behaviors during times of stress. They can use their emotional intelligence more acutely and in a targeted fashion to learn from life's setbacks and cope more effectively. Resilient people understand the benefits associated with positive emotions and use this awareness to their advantage when coping with negative emotional events.[10]

Currently, a quarter of all employees view their jobs as the number one stressor in their lives, according to the Centers for Disease Control and Prevention.[11] Workplace stress results in 120,000 premature deaths per year, and related treatment costs account for 5 to 8 percent of total annual national healthcare costs.[12] Personal challenges can also trickle into the workplace. Studies have shown that a large portion of employees who either get terminated or voluntarily resign from their jobs do so because of personal stressors like terminal illness or the loss of a loved one. New research from BetterUp—an online leadership development company—has found that people with low resilience are four times more likely to experience burnout.[13] The case for increasing resilience is clear. Promoting emotional resilience for employees can directly impact their overall productivity and help them maintain a better quality of life.

WHAT IS RESILIENCE?

Resilience is a characteristic that can be taught. More than fifty years of research show that resilience is built by attitudes, behaviors, and social supports that can be adopted and cultivated by anyone. Factors that lead to resilience include optimism, the ability to stay balanced and manage strong or difficult emotions, a sense of safety, and a strong social support system.

Being resilient doesn't mean that you won't encounter problems or have difficulty overcoming challenges in your life. The difference is that resilient people don't let their adversity *define* them. At its core, resilience is about being capable and strong enough to persevere in adverse or stressful conditions—and to take away positive meaning from that experience.[14] Resilience is the ability to cope with challenges and thrive under adversity rather than ruminating and obsessing over them.[15]

Emotional resilience is the way through which we empower ourselves to perceive adversities as "temporary" and keep evolving through the pain and sufferings. It is an intertwined combination of self-awareness, situational acknowledgment, self-belief, hope, and committed action. It means bouncing back from a stressful encounter and not letting it affect our internal motivation. It is not a "bend but don't break" trait; rather, resilience is accepting that "I am broken" and continuing to grow with the broken pieces put back together. The most resilient individuals and teams aren't the ones that don't fail but the ones that fail, learn, and thrive because of it.

Academic research into resilience started over fifty years ago with pioneering studies by Norman Garmezy, professor emeritus at the University of Minnesota. After studying why many children of schizophrenic parents did not suffer psychological illness as a result of growing up with their parents, he concluded that a certain quality of resilience played a greater role in mental health than anyone had previously suspected.[16]

More recently, there was a study published in 2003 that focused on the resilience of college students.[17] The study began in August 2001, one month prior to the 9/11 tragedy. This gave researchers a unique opportunity to deepen their insights about resilience and coping after such a tragic event. Participants who had scored high on resilience prior to the attacks reported greater positive emotions such as gratitude, interest, and love, even while simultaneously feeling negative emotions such as fear, anger, and sadness. Researchers also found that these highly resilient people increased their levels of optimism, well-being, and feelings of tranquility and peace after 9/11.

This study illustrates how resilient people not only bounce back from hard times but also grow and become stronger as a result—they experience post-traumatic growth. They found a way for their struggle to redefine their life and fill it with new meaning. These individuals emerge from otherwise awful experiences because they allow themselves to notice value and opportunity where they may have never seen them before. This type of growth is the cornerstone of resilience.[18]

FROM TRAUMA TO TRIUMPH

Harvard Medical School professor of psychiatry Judith Herman calls trauma "the affliction of the powerless."[19] The problem is we're all powerless against the vicissitudes of fate. "At the moment of trauma, the victim is rendered helpless by an overwhelming force. When the force is that of nature, we speak of disasters. When the force is that of other human beings, we speak of atrocities," she writes in her book *Trauma and Recovery.* "Traumatic events are extraordinary, not because they occur rarely, but rather because they overwhelm the ordinary human adaptations to life." Depending on the particular type of trauma, about a quarter of survivors will fall into post-traumatic stress disorder, a painful and often debilitating condition. Others will experience significant depression or anxiety.

Suffering is real, but resilience is also real. It is an incredible and encouraging fact about human nature that, contrary to popular belief, after a period of emotional turmoil, most trauma survivors eventually recover and return to their lives. They bounce back. And in some cases, they do much more. They bounce *forward* in truly remarkable ways. "A significant minority, as a result of the trauma, feel called upon to engage in a wider world," writes Herman. They focus their energies on a new calling, on a new mission, on a new path, on helping others who have been victimized, on education, on legal reforms, or any number of other big goals.[20]

According to research, most post-traumatic growth is internal and private. Survivors report they've changed for the better, and they may feel the benefits of that change, but outwardly their lives don't look much different from before the trauma. Perceived growth isn't fake, however. Though the research is mixed, some studies show links between greater perceived growth and lower emotional distress as well as better physical health.[21]

In their book, *Supersurvivors: The Surprising Link Between Suffering and Success,* Feldman and Kravetz share several true stories of how ordinary people accomplished extraordinary things after experiencing trauma.[22] From a leukemia sufferer who won an Olympic gold medal to a blind man who rowed across the Atlantic Ocean to a woman who survived genocide and went on to become one of President Obama's appointees, "supersurvivors" radically deviated from their life path, transforming the worst thing to happen into their best success. Turning tragedy intro triumph encompasses the following steps:

1. Confront reality
2. Reflect deeply
3. Face the stark realities and worst-case scenarios
4. Grieve what never will be

5. Disengage from previous goals
6. Create new goals
7. Believe in yourself
8. Take risks
9. Move toward new goal achievement
10. Celebrate your successes and learn from your failures

While some people have an easier time turning trauma into triumphs, resilience is a skill we can all develop. It is not a fixed state of being.[23] We can build resilience and continue to work on it just like we can train our brain to be more positive and optimistic. Positive emotions play a large role in resilience. Research has shown that they help us rebound better from trauma and find opportunities for growth from stressful experiences.[24]

Studies have indicated that resilient individuals can deal with stress more effectively. They can bounce back from any stressful situation with positive energy and confidence, and they are more likely to learn lessons from traumatic encounters rather than get overwhelmed by them.[25] According to Diane Contu, author of "How Resilience Works," resilient people possess three defining characteristics: (1) they accept the harsh realities facing them, (2) they find meaning in hardship, and (3) they have an uncanny ability to improvise, making do with whatever's at hand instead of crying out in despair.[26]

At the heart of the transformation from trauma to triumph is a person's mindset and their commitment to moving forward. Perseverance is the steadfastness to hold onto your course of action, while resilience is the ability to adapt to stress quickly and be strengthened by our challenges.[27] While perseverance is a noble quality, giving up can sometimes be better than persisting.

At Concordia University, psychologist Carsten Wrosch has extensively researched the finer points of giving up. "The notion that persistence is essential for success is deeply embedded within American culture," he writes with coauthor Gregory Miller in the journal *Psychological Science*.[28] But there are times when doggedly pursuing a goal may hurt more than it helps. "Specifically, when people find themselves in situations in which they are unlikely to realize a goal, the most adaptive responsive may be to disengage from it. By withdrawing from a goal that is unattainable, a person can avoid repeated failure experiences and their consequences for mind and body."[29]

Goal disengagement doesn't mean lowering one's standards. It simply means beginning the goal pursuit process from where we are rather than deluding ourselves or denying the reality of our situation. It means spending time on goals that are possible given our capabilities, limitations, and resources. This is a better recipe for fulfillment than striving for impossible dreams.[30]

A common belief about resilience is that it stems from an optimistic nature, which is true only if optimism doesn't distort your sense of reality. In adverse situations, distorted overly optimistic thinking, with no regard for potential risks, can be disastrous. People who focus on the positives while avoiding identification of potential negatives, or those who believe that everything is, or will be, fine despite there being actual risk, may not take appropriate action to protect themselves. Their lack of belief in their own susceptibility may be dangerous.

Research suggests that most people slip into denial as a coping mechanism. When we take a sober, down-to-earth view of the reality of our situation, however grueling that may be, we prepare ourselves to act in ways that allow us to endure and survive extraordinary hardship. We train ourselves how to survive before the fact. This is hard to do when we insist on thinking only positive thoughts.

In *Supersurvivors*, what makes their stories of survival special is their ability to stop thinking positively and start thinking realistically, to avoid the comforting fiction that "everything will be fine" and instead bravely ask, "What now?" Denying or distorting a bad situation may be comforting in the short term, but it's potentially harmful in the long run. Giving up on an unattainable goal and creating a new goal that motivates and inspires you to action is the only way to move forward. Truly accepting the consequences of a trauma and adopting realistic thinking rather than delusional positive thinking can open you up to true hope—something that enables setting and achieving goals that ultimately can improve one's life.[31] This research provides a foundation to understand how increased resilience can help us navigate the twists and turns of our careers, including listening to and acting upon critical feedback.

DEALING WITH CRITICISM

Nobody likes performance reviews, and rarely do people proactively ask for feedback. Why do people avoid feedback? Because we hate being criticized. Employees are terrified they'll hear nothing but criticism from their manager. Managers often think their direct reports will respond to even the mildest criticism with blame, denial, anger, or tears. As a result, people often take the path of least resistance by saying as little as possible. However, feedback is a gift that people don't have to give.

Both the thought of critical feedback and the actual receiving of feedback during performance review or in the course of day-to-day pressures and demands can send people into a destructive psychological tailspin. Fears and assumptions can lead to destructive behaviors that negatively affect not only our work but the overall health of our organizations.[32] Behaviors include

1. Procrastination. We procrastinate—usually consciously—when we feel helpless about a situation and are anxious, embarrassed, or otherwise dissatisfied with it. Procrastination commonly contains an element of hostility or anger.
2. Denial. We're in denial when we're unable or unwilling to face reality or fail to acknowledge the implications of our situations.
3. Brooding. Brooding is a powerful emotional response, taking the form of morbid preoccupation and a sense of foreboding. Faced with situations they feel they can't master, brooders lapse into passivity, paralysis, and isolation.
4. Jealousy. This becomes maladaptive when it is based on suspicion, rivalry, envy, or possessiveness.
5. Self-Sabotage. Workplaces are full of people who unconsciously undercut themselves.

If you are committed to improving your performance and advancing your career, it is critical to become comfortable both asking for and receiving feedback, including strengths, natural talents, and constructive criticism. Getting a well-rounded perspective helps you discover where you're especially strong and uncovers blind spots that may be preventing you from making your desired impact on people and your organization's goals and objectives.

It's a good practice to get 360 feedback annually within the workplace. Respondents should include subordinates, peers, your manager, and others who may not be in your team or organization. If you want to get a deeper appreciation of how people see you, include people outside of your organization. This can include family members, friends, mentors, and other trusted people in your network. While conversations are beneficial, written feedback is most impactful. This includes answering questions in a scale and/or providing verbatim comments. People are naturally biased toward listening for the good and denying and/or defending the bad. Memorializing feedback in a written document gives the individual time to process the feedback and engage in the inherent emotional journey. Feedback deepens self-awareness, prompts reflection, and illuminates opportunities for growth in both the what (technical skills) and the how (soft skills). When you receive feedback, you can accept it, reject it, or simply look at it as a data point from someone else's perspective. Either way, remember that feedback is a gift, so be sure to say thank you.

When it comes to providing feedback to others, I often ask others about their own self-assessment. This helps to assess a person's level of self-awareness and often eases the tension that naturally arises when the manager is the only person providing feedback. For those with high self-awareness, sometimes feedback from others is an acknowledgment of what we already know to be true about ourselves but may not have openly admitted. Whether positive or constructive, it is typically easier to accept because it affirms our beliefs. However, accepting feedback that was not apparent to you requires ruthless self-honesty and reflection.

On my first day of college, my professor taught our class that perception is reality. Whether we agree or disagree, what others observe, experience, and feel is real to them. Instead of judging whether someone is right or wrong, I've learned to make peace with how other people see things and to see their conclusions as *valid*. Once we understand the feedback, it's up to us if and how we choose to respond. If you're not ready to respond to feedback, or you want time to fully process it, thank the feedback provider and indicate that you will get back to them with a plan of action after you've had time to absorb what you've heard. Acting on feedback is the sign of a great leader. The following are strategies to build emotional resilience.

PRACTICAL STRATEGIES TO
BUILD EMOTIONAL RESILIENCE

1. *Practice mindfulness.* Become keenly aware of the circumstances, how you feel, what you think, and what your options are. Self-awareness is the ability to tune into your feelings, internal conflicts, and perception of the world. Through self-awareness, you gain a deeper understanding of how feelings contribute to your actions.

Separating your thoughts from your feelings empowers you to think before acting and respond instead of reacting. It also gives you time and space to face the realities, identify the source of stress, and explore potential solutions to move forward. You can only reflect once you've become detached from the raw emotions. Not to be confused with being insensitive or aloof, being detached is avoiding hypersensitivity, which enables you to view the situation as a third-party observer. Creating a one-second mental space between an event or stimulus and your response to it can be the difference between making a rushed decision that leads to failure and reaching a thoughtful conclusion that leads to increased performance. It's the difference between acting out of anger and applying due patience. It's a one-second lead over your mind, your emotions, and your world that empowers you to approach the future with high intent and low attachment.[33]

"Decentering" stress is not denying or suppressing that we feel stressed; rather, it is the process of being able to pause, to observe the experience from a neutral standpoint, and then to try to solve the problem. When we can cognitively take a step back from our experience and label our thoughts and emotions, we are effectively pivoting attention from the neural network in our brains to the more observational parts of our brains. Being mentally agile and decentering stress when it occurs enables the core resilience skill of "response flexibility," which renowned psychologist Linda Graham described as the ability to "find ways to respond to a trigger or a stressor with new behaviors rather than out of automatic, reactive habits, to shift perspectives, create options, and choose among them wisely."[34]

2. *Breathe slowly and deeply.* Diaphragmatic breathing has numerous benefits; it

- Helps self-regulation
- Lowers heart rate
- Lowers blood pressure
- Slows down your physical response and helps avoid the fight-or-flight response
- Helps you relax
- Lowers the harmful effects of the stress hormone cortisol on your body
- Improves your core muscle stability
- Improves your body's ability to tolerate intense exercise
- Lowers your chances of injuring or wearing out your muscles
- Slows your rate of breathing so that you expend less energy
- Reduces stress [35]

Being stressed keeps your immune system from working at full capacity. This can make you more susceptible to numerous health conditions. Over time, chronic stress, even from seemingly minor inconveniences like traffic, issues with loved ones, or other daily concerns, can cause you to develop anxiety or depression. Some deep breathing exercises can help you reduce these effects of stress. Here are the basic procedures for diaphragmatic breathing:

- Sit in a comfortable position or lie flat on the floor, your bed, or another comfortable, flat surface.
- Relax your shoulders.
- Put a hand on your chest and a hand on your stomach.
- Breathe in through your nose for about two seconds. You should experience the air moving through your nostrils into your abdomen, making your stomach expand. During this type of breathing, make sure your stomach is moving outward while your chest remains relatively still.
- Purse your lips (as if you're about to drink through a straw), press gently on your stomach, and exhale slowly for about two seconds.
- Repeat these steps several times for best results.

Diaphragmatic breathing is beneficial in high-stress situations and as a daily practice to stay grounded and in greater control of your response to life's inevitable curveballs.

3. *Build a robust emotional vocabulary.* Everyone experiences emotions. The purpose of expressing emotions is to help you reach a resolution to what's bothering you. This can't be done if your feelings are bottled up or unexpressed. There are dozens of words for different emotions. Being able to articulate and understand the subtle distinctions between various emotions, for example, being irritable, upset, or anxious, is called emotional granularity. A person with low emotional granularity describes feelings with generic words such as "good" or "mad." Studies show that when we learn to distinguish among specific emotions both within ourselves and in others, we are less likely to react without thinking and more likely to think through our options before acting on our emotions or the situation.[36]

Research shows that translating feelings into even just one or two words literally calms the part of our brain that controls emotions, which greatly reduces our emotions' influence over us.[37] Search the internet for a list of emotions and feelings to better understand the variety and nuances of emotions.

4. *Reflect.* As you process the situation, it's healthy to reflect but not to ruminate. Churning over the if-onlys about the past or being anxious over the what-ifs of the future is futile. Here are thought starters for your reflection:

- Take responsibility for any words, actions, and behaviors that may have affected the situation.
- Consider how the new circumstance affects your current and future goals.
- Draw on experiences from the past as a frame of reference for the current situation.
- Keep your values at the forefront and resist the urge to act out of character.
- Articulate what you have learned that will make you stronger and wiser in the future.

- Identify concerns quickly and courageously; don't let them fester.
- Explore the possibilities and consider the potential upsides of this unforeseen situation.

5. *Reframe your mindset.* You can view the setback as a challenge instead of a threat and also as a new opportunity instead of an unwelcome, unfortunate fate. A cognitive appraisal of challenges focuses on the possibility that growth or some good can and will come from adverse situations. It comes with the perception that you have the capacity and resources to cope with the situation. In contrast, threat appraisals mean you're viewing the situation as beyond your ability to cope with it, triggering fear, anxiety, and anger and leading to fight, flight, or freeze reactions. Energy is derailed away from problem solving to emotionally coping.[38] One simple way to reframe your mindset is to stop thinking as a victim and instead think in terms of victory (see table 6.1).

Table 6.1. Reframing Your Mindset

Victim Mentality	Victorious Mentality
There's nothing I can do.	I will take control of what I can influence.
I can't adjust.	I will give it a good-faith effort.
This will never end.	I've seen worse times passing.
I can never move on.	I will give this situation some time.
My future is uncertain.	Today, I am grateful for . . .
Change is happening *to me*.	I choose how I respond.

Research has found that super-resilient people are six times more likely to do one thing: force themselves to have an internal locus of control. In other words, the more you believe that you have control over the outcomes of your life (and that you can cope with less than optimal outcomes), the more resilient you are. In contrast, according to the researchers, "the more external the locus of control, the more people tend to feel victimized by the events of the world and the less likely they will be to help themselves. The truth is, you only get to be a victim once. After that, you're a volunteer. So, when it's time to cope, to bounce back in the face of adversity, ask yourself, 'Do I just want to change, or do *I* want to change it?' The former is how a victim thinks, the latter indicates you're ready to make your victim mentality a victim."[39]

Rather than looking for help or blaming the world for our miseries, combining self-awareness with a victory mindset gives us the courage to assume control of what may feel like a hopeless, uncontrollable situation.

6. *Search for Meaning.* Resist any impulse to view yourself as a victim and to cry, "Why me?" Instead, reframe your suffering to create greater meaning for yourself and others. Finding meaning is the way resilient people build bridges from present-day hardships to a fuller life and better-constructed future. Those bridges make the present manageable, for lack of a better word, removing the sense that the present is overwhelming.

In his book *Man's Search for Meaning*, Austrian psychiatrist and Auschwitz survivor and author Viktor Frankl described the pivotal moment in the camp when he developed meaning therapy. He was on his way to work one day, worrying about whether he should trade his last cigarette for a bowl of soup. He wondered how he was going to work with a new foreman whom he knew to be particularly sadistic. Suddenly, he was disgusted by just how trivial and meaningless his life had become. He realized that to survive, he had to find some purpose. Frankl did so by imagining himself giving a lecture after the war on the psychology of the concentration camp to help outsiders understand what he had been through. Although he wasn't even sure he would survive, Frankl created concrete goals for himself. In doing so, he succeeded in rising above the sufferings of the moment. As he put it in his book: "We must never forget that we may also find meaning in life even when confronted with a hopeless situation, when facing a fate that cannot be changed."[40]

7. *Forgive.* One of the world's foremost researchers on hope, University of Kansas psychologist C. R. Snyder helped to develop a prominent theory of forgiveness. "Forgiveness is giving up

the hope that the past could be any different," he was fond of saying.[41] Forgiveness means breaking the psychological ties that bind you to the past and giving up the quest to change what has already happened. Sometimes giving up on impossible goals can free people to experience true hope, the *grounded* hope of changing the future. Having a realistic view of the situation and a strong view of one's ability to control one's destiny through one's efforts leads to grounded hope, and more hope leads to greater goal attainment.

Along with psychologist Laura Yamhure Thompson and a team of researchers, Snyder created a psychological test to measure forgiveness, called the Heartland Forgiveness Scale. In a 2005 study appearing in the *Journal of Personality*, they report strong correlations between this test, hope, and depression.[42]

Archbishop Desmond Tutu famously said, "Without forgiveness, there is no hope." He was referring to South Africa immediately following the abolition of apartheid, encouraging a resistance to seeking revenge upon white leaders who formerly perpetrated human rights violations against the black majority. Though research on the topic is still in its infancy, forgiveness may play a more important role in nurturing hope than anyone ever thought. Psychologist Loren Toussaint at Luther College in Iowa, along with his colleagues David Williams, Marc Musick, and Susan Everson-Rose, analyzed more than 1,400 telephone interviews across the United States. Toussaint and his colleagues found that hope may be the link between forgiveness and lowered risk of depression. They also found that less willingness to forgive predicted greater hopelessness, which in turn predicted greater depression.[43]

Forgiveness is a powerful tool that restores relationships, leads to inner peace, and helps people to engage in many aspects of emotional intelligence. Forgiveness is often necessary when there is internal or external tension and conflict that needs to be resolved. That small voice or nagging feeling in your gut creates an opportunity to reflect, which will deepen emotional self-awareness, empathy, social awareness, and can lead to emotional self-control. As Tutu once said, "Without forgiveness, there can be no future for a relationship between individuals or within and between nations."

Forgiveness is both for the forgiver and the forgiven. According to Toussaint et al.'s results, people's answers to the forgiveness questions were among the best predictors of their probability of having depression.[44] It's not surprising that people's tendency to forgive themselves for wrongdoing they've perpetrated against others is associated with a lower probability of encountering depression. Guilt and shame can be depressing. More surprising, people who tended to forgive *others* for wronging them also appeared to enjoy lowered probability of depression.[45]

Forgiveness is not limited to religious people who believe in a higher power. Dozens of studies have documented the benefits to laypeople of religion and spirituality in coping with a variety of life stressors, including cancer, heart failure, kidney failure, depression, obesity, serious mental illness, and even the daily hassles of ordinary life. While nobody is scientifically claiming that being nonreligious is a detriment to one's mental or physical health, having a genuine sense of faith appears, in many cases, to be a very good thing.[46]

8. *Engage your support network.* Research shows that extroverted individuals tend to be more resilient because they're more likely to reach out to others when they need support. Asking for coaching as part of that support network has been proven to build resilience.[47] Coaching doesn't always come from your manager or someone above your level. Some of the best coaching comes from peers, especially if you've built relationships that are more collaborative than competitive.

The power that comes with the hierarchy of being a subordinate to your boss or an employee of yours inevitably impacts how people engage with you. However, the dynamic of power is different. Like siblings, peers often see you when you're at your best and when you're at your worst. Their brand perceptions of you are also established through formal and informal settings, such as meetings, hallway conversation, and text/instant messages. Therefore, unlike your boss or employees, they often have a more balanced point of view because of those diverse experiences. Spouses, family members, and significant others also serve as an excellent source of feedback for many of the same reasons noted above.

9. *Take control of your outcomes.* It is difficult to control your emotions; however, emotions can be managed through techniques such as

- Pausing—Count to ten and take a deep breath. This gives you time to process the situation, identify how you feel, and form a thoughtful response. It also helps you to avoid acting before you think and drawing misguided conclusions.
- Being slow to speak—Don't feel the need to fill up space with words. Emotional self-control includes getting comfortable with silence.
- Believing that you control your destiny—Successful people believe that they have the internal capacity to make desirable things happen. They see opportunities where others see threats, and much of this belief is driven by their mindset.
- Taking calculated risks—In many cases, when it comes to bouncing forward after a trauma and doing great things, the aforementioned supersurvivors adopted a bit of overconfidence and a slightly skewed perception of risk. Many of us are "smart" and never attempt half the crazy things they did. However, we also never achieve their elevated successes, even though we might be perfectly capable of doing so.[48]

10. *Express gratitude.* Learning to appreciate what we have and who we are, instead of complaining and stressing about what we don't have or who we think we should be, is a powerful technique to redirect stressful, negative emotions. Consider the following gratitude thought starters:

- I'm grateful for _____.
- I'm grateful that _____ didn't happen.
- I'm grateful _____ happened to me.
- I'm grateful I accomplished these goals: _____.

- I'm grateful to have _____ in my life.
- I'm grateful that I am _____.
- I'm grateful that I am not _____.

EMOTIONAL INTELLIGENCE INSIGHTS

41. Leaders are deeply human and, therefore, deeply imperfect.
A title in an organization doesn't transform a human being into being divine. On the contrary, growing in leadership requires gaining clarity of your strengths and deficiencies. Be committed to a positive future by taking intentional steps that neutralize weaknesses and manage destructive emotions that can harm your brand, reduce your confidence, and diminish your effectiveness.

> *"A wise leader surrounds themselves with experts*
> *who fortify their areas of weakness."*

42. Agility is about making tweaks without sacrificing authenticity.

Every time there's a change in your job, team members, manager, or leaders, a new dynamic is created.

> *"Surviving and thriving despite constant change requires*
> *agility in your approach, alliances, priorities, and actions."*

When you feel like you're "losing yourself" in the sea of change, ask yourself if the fit is still mutual. If the answer is no, move on gracefully with a heart of gratitude, not blame or shame.

43. Leadership can be lonely.
Leadership is fraught with tough decisions. Out of confidentiality and respect for others, leaders can't always fully explain situations to everyone. This can lead to being misunderstood, blamed, falsely accused, or judged. Sometimes, even those who've been most loyal can abandon you.

> *"When you know in your heart that you've done your best, encourage*
> *yourself, seek support from confidantes, and walk with integrity."*

44. Friends and "work friends" are not synonymous.

"Work is like a game of chess.
You're making moves with an endgame in mind."

Since information is currency, be thoughtful about how much you share and experience with coworkers. Organizational change can happen in an instant, and when someone feels like a "checkmate" is on the horizon, what you do and say could be used against you. Be friendly at work, and nurture deeper friendships with people outside of work.

45. Self-worth is not defined by your job or your boss.
You have been created for a divine purpose, and your profession often plays a large part in fulfilling this purpose.

"Your job shouldn't define you."

During times when you are less motivated or feel that your gifts aren't being fully utilized at work, give some of your time and energy to employee networks, community service, and other activities that feed your soul and bring you joy. Look with optimism toward a more hopeful future.

46. The fit isn't always mutual.
Sometimes the way you see yourself and the way the organization sees you don't match. Signs of misalignment include personality conflicts, stalled progression, marginalized roles, indirect or nonexistent feedback, and an unsettling feeling. Soul-searching will help you decide if you want to invest the physical, mental, and emotional energy to stay.

"Sometimes you have to go if you want to grow."

· 7 ·

Mastering Emotional Self-Management

*F*ailure is inevitable on the road to success. Some of the most successful people, myself included, have experienced tremendous loss, disappointment, detours, and, yes, even failures. Success isn't limited to the smartest people with the highest IQs. Success comes to those who are driven to succeed. When you have clarity in who you are and where you're going and are willing to pivot when necessary to reach your desired destination despite the obstacles, chances are that you will experience your share of success. There are numerous examples of notable people whose visible success was shaped by perseverance and determination to succeed despite repeated failures.

Walt Disney, iconic animator, filmmaker, and theme park developer, experienced many failures: he was traumatized as a child by an abusive father; his first cartoon business went bankrupt; he failed as an actor; he was swindled by a producer who took legal rights to his animations; his Mickey Mouse concept was rejected by bankers over three hundred times before one person said yes; and he had a nervous breakdown after an employer stole his longtime and best animator from him. But he didn't let these repeated business and personal challenges stop him. Disney tried something new and pivoted his business model to enter the movie industry. Introduced in 1937, *Snow White and the Seven Dwarfs* is still a classic today. However, that was soon followed by movies that weren't as successful at the time but are household names today: *Pinocchio* (1940), *Fantasia* (1940), and *Bambi* (1942).[1]

Disney's debt was nearly $4 million by the end of World War II, exacerbated by his animators going on strike. When the war ended, his company was slow to rebuild. So he diversified his business once again, moving into television despite advice by producers to stay focused on films. This led to great success with TV shows like *The Mickey Mouse Club* and *Davy Crockett*. This impressive turnaround enabled Disney to diversify the business even further with the development of Disneyland, the "happiest place on Earth." However, this wasn't the end of his failures.

Disneyland opened on July 17, 1955, in Anaheim, California, but the day soon became known as "Black Sunday." Tickets were forged, leading to lines that trailed seven miles long. Temperatures were nearly 100 degrees, causing women's high heels to melt in the new asphalt. A plumber's strike left drinking fountains inoperable, and some of the rides malfunctioned. But that didn't stop Walt Disney. He learned and course-corrected from these failures and went on to be one of the world's most iconic visionaries in the entertainment industry. It all started with an abused child who took solace in drawing.

Commenting on the benefits of failure, Disney once said: "All the adversity I've had in my life, all the troubles and obstacles, have strengthened me. You may not realize it when it happens, but a kick in the teeth may be the best thing in the world for you."

Milton Hershey, founder of the Hershey Company, also has a compelling story of perseverance that took him from failures to fortunes. The only surviving child of Veronica "Fanny" Snavely and Henry Hershey, his father left the family in their rural farming community when Milton was an adolescent. He dropped out of school at thirteen years old and expressed an interest in candy making. He began apprenticing with a master confectioner in Lancaster, Pennsylvania. With this knowledge, he opened and operated a candy store in Philadelphia, Pennsylvania, for five years but eventually closed up shop. After traveling to Denver, Colorado, to reunite with his father, Milton began working with a confectioner where he discovered caramel and how fresh milk could be used to make it.[2]

Hershey failed at attempts to sell his caramels in both Chicago and New York and returned to his hometown in Derry Township, Pennsylvania, at the age of twenty-six. He perfected his business and success soon followed with customers all over the country. Always open to learning and growing, he got a firsthand view of the art of chocolate making at the World's Columbian Exposition in Chicago in 1893. He was intrigued and sprang into action. With a growing caramel business, he started Hershey Chocolate Company. During an era when chocolate was largely concentrated in Switzerland, Hershey learned to mass-produce and mass-distribute milk chocolate candy.

In 1900, he sold Lancaster Caramel Company for $1 million, which is the equivalent of nearly $30 million today. The success of Hershey's Chocolate Company is unrivaled. In 1907, the Hershey's Kiss was introduced. During my time as an employee of what is now known as The Hershey Company, I was honored to serve as director of Hershey's KISSES®, an iconic global brand and household name. The company's portfolio includes many well-known brands, such as Hershey's®, Reese's®, Twizzlers®, and Jolly Rancher®.

Mr. Hershey, as employees called him, was very benevolent. During World War II, Hershey supplied military forces with chocolate bars called the Ration D Bar and the better-tasting Tropical Chocolate Bar. He built schools, parks, churches, recreational facilities, and housing for his employees, a model community that became known as Hershey, Pennsylvania, "the sweetest place on Earth." He even added a trolley system for his workers that still operates.

Unable to have children of their own, Milton and his wife, Catherine Hershey, opened the Hershey Industrial School in 1909, a facility for orphaned boys. It is now known as the Milton Hershey School, a home for underprivileged boys and girls from prekindergarten through twelfth grade. An intimate community, nearly two thousand students live on campus in 160 student homes of eight to twelve students plus house parents during the school year, breaks, and summer vacations. Admission is totally free to families who qualify for enrollment, which includes housing, meals, extracurricular activities, clothing, school supplies, medical and dental care, and much more.[3]

In 1918, three years after his wife's unexpected death, Mr. Hershey transferred much of his wealth, which included his ownership of the Hershey Chocolate Company, to the Hershey Trust, which is designed to fund the Milton Hershey School in perpetuity. Mr. Hershey was a humble man, and that culture still permeates across the company and throughout the town. Keep buying Hershey products—a portion of every dollar you spend helps to sustain this world-class institution.

His philanthropic nature was persistent even through challenging economic times. In the 1930s, during the Great Depression, Hershey infused capital into his town to construct new offices for the Hershey

Company, a community building, and the Hershey Hotel, a beautiful, world-class facility. Hershey has become a destination for tourists from all over the world. None of this would have been possible had it not been for the persistence, work ethic, and ingenuity of Mr. Hershey to keep going despite the obstacles.

These business titans aren't the only people who have experienced failure yet persevered until they succeeded:

- **The Beatles** nearly broke up after an unsuccessful audition with the leading record company of their era, Decca Records. Dick Rowe, head of Decca, predicted "guitar groups are on the way out." He's probably eaten those words.[4] The Beatles went on to be named by *Rolling Stone* as the best artist of all time and have sold more units in the United States than any other artist, according to the Recording Industry Association of America.[5]
- **Lady Gaga** was told that she wasn't marketable and that none of the songs she made were hits. After being rejected from multiple record companies, she was signed as an artist with Island Def Jam Records but was unexplainably dropped three months later. She turned to drinking and drugs to cope, but she never gave up. She tweaked her personal image without losing her authenticity, kept writing new songs, and was eventually signed by Interscope Records. She has become one of the best-selling artists in recent history in terms of both record sales and tour revenue, as well as being a recipient of five Grammy awards and other accolades.[6]
- **Steve Jobs** was fired from the very company he began. The dismissal made him realize that his passion for work exceeded the disappointment of failure. Further ventures such as NeXT and Pixar eventually led Jobs back to the CEO position at Apple. "I didn't see it then, but it turned out that getting fired from Apple was the best thing that could have ever happened to me," commented Jobs.[7]
- **Michael Jordan** wasn't naturally built for basketball in his early years. Basketball coaches had trouble looking past his height, which didn't meet the minimum standards. However, that didn't stop Jordan. "I've missed more than 9,000 shots in my career. I've lost almost 300 games. Twenty-six times, I've been trusted to take the game-winning shot and missed. I've

failed over and over and over again in my life. And that is why I succeed," said Jordan.[8] Jordan is one of the greatest basketball players of all time.

- **Oprah** had a less than desirable childhood. Born in rural Mississippi to a teenage mother, she was abused from the age of nine, ran away from home at thirteen, became pregnant at fourteen, and lost her baby shortly after birth. However, once she moved to Tennessee to live with her father, she turned her life around. After earning a full ride and graduating from Tennessee State University, she landed a job as a coanchor of the evening news in Baltimore, Maryland. However, neither her cohost nor the community were receptive to her, and she was demoted to a job she didn't enjoy. Winfrey called these early years the "first and worst failure of her TV career," but she had an epiphany. Oprah discovered that she loved television but hated television news. She enjoyed covering human interest stories but couldn't stay emotionally detached. And while she thrived in the role of host, she was unable to do so with a cohost unless they had a deep connection.[9] These experiences prepared her to cohost a talk show, which eventually led to the creation of the iconic *The Oprah Winfrey Show*, one of the longest running daytime TV talk shows in history. She is the recipient of forty-six Daytime Emmy Awards.[10]

What separates those who succeed from those who fail?

1. *Vision:* You've got to see it before you see it, or you never will see it. The vision of where you can be and who you can become is a motivating factor to persevere. People who vividly describe or picture their goals are anywhere from 1.2 to 1.4 times more likely to successfully accomplish their goals than people who don't.[11] Write the vision and make it plain, whether on a napkin, your career development plan, business plan, or vision board.

2. *Internal fortitude:* Encouragement from others may inspire you and stir up optimistic feelings, but fortitude is a motivating force that comes from within. It's the strength of mind, firmness of purpose, and resolve to dig in and make things happen. This type of grit separates the victors from the victims.

3. *Self-confidence:* Even if others don't believe in you or see your vision, if you believe in yourself and work harder than most, chances are that you will accomplish your goals. Having self-confidence means managing your inner world, including your thoughts, feelings, self-talk, and that pesky inner critic. Not to be confused with being egocentric, self-confidence is being clear about your strengths, natural talents, and areas of opportunity. In areas of weakness, self-confidence is asking for help, delegating, and/or being intentional about neutralizing the weakness.

4. *Continuous learning:* No failure is wasted if you learn and grow from it. Assess what worked and what didn't work, what you learned, and what you would do next time, preferably in writing to drive the most clarity and closure. Then, demonstrate compassion for yourself and others through forgiveness. When you're more committed to the outcome than how hard the process may be, you are sure to come out of the situation wiser for having tried, even if you fail.

5. *Risk tolerance:* As the adage goes, if at first you don't succeed, try, try, and try again. Bouncing back from failure requires a combination of curiosity, belief, and risk-taking. For people who are driven to succeed, it is better to try and fail than to never have tried and to let the idea die inside of you.

The stories above highlight transformative, often traumatic failures that changed the course of these leaders' lives and shaped the person they were meant to be. However, there are plenty of less dramatic failures and disruptions that cause us to pivot. Navigating a career is an unpredictable journey. On the road to success, it's inevitable that we will encounter detours and roadblocks such as company politics, changes to organizational structures, lack of access and rapport with key influencers, shifting priorities and success metrics, feeling marginalized, self-doubt, and more. If you're a people leader, it gets even more complicated. While managing the highs and lows of our own careers, we're also responsible for leading, motivating, and influencing our teams to accomplish the organization's goals despite these challenges.

Some failures are self-induced, some are avoidable, and others are unintentional. Sometimes it's caused by what we do or don't do—a mistake, blunder, or error; other times, it can *feel* like we're a failure—not being selected for the role, being downsized, or falling out of favor with others. In any circumstance, emotional self-awareness and agility helps us to more quickly navigate the difficulties of life.

Several years ago, in a leadership development course, I heard an acronym describing the business market that has certainly come to pass: VUCA, which stands for volatile, uncertain, complex, and ambiguous. I have worked in three industries—consumer packaged goods, confection, and healthcare—at three different Fortune 500 companies—Procter & Gamble, The Hershey Company, and Cardinal Health. Over time, these VUCA attributes have intensified in these and other industries and companies. Global trade and economic policies create volatility and uncertainty. The number of mergers, acquisitions, consolidations, and buyouts has accelerated. Financial pressure and acquisition financials have led to job cuts and other types of consolidation. As of 2016, millennials became the largest generation in the workforce,[12] yet they are less loyal than other generational counterparts, causing higher turnover rates. Disruption has become the norm, with startups and alternative business models disrupting long-standing businesses and brands. It is definitely a VUCA world.

Clay Christensen, noted researcher, author, and professor at Harvard University, developed a business theory called disruptive innovation, an approach intended to disrupt established market-leading firms, products, and alliances.[13] One of my most interesting assignments at Procter & Gamble (P&G) was as the innovation manager for Align, a revolutionary probiotic for digestive wellness. P&G is known for its brand management discipline and success with household brands like Crest, Tide, Dawn, Swiffer, Olay, Pantene, and Secret. Unlike most P&G product innovation, which is vetted through extensive lab research, consumer testing, and modeling, disruptive innovation is a slower, more methodical process that identifies assumptions and activates tests to prove or disprove the assumption. Without going into extensive detail, the Align brand spent several years in test markets, and the team validated the most important details of the proposition before the mass launch. I was on the team that validated the in-market sales velocity, which is units per store per week. The brand exceeded pilot market success metrics and launched nationwide. More than ten years later, Align is still on the market, an impressive statistic since 95 percent of new products fail.[14]

I've spent about half of my career in general management roles at for-profit businesses and the other half in product innovation roles—some of the products succeeded and others didn't sustain past a few years. One critical attribute that separates traditional innovation from disruptive innovation is the willingness to pivot. When you learn what works and what doesn't, are you willing to make the necessary adjustments for greater success? Do you anticipate what the competition might do, and how you can preempt them or respond? Are you staying in tune with your customers' needs and desires and exceeding their expectations?

There are so many examples of innovation that has disrupted established players and changed the game. Often, it boils down to a simple question that illuminated a customer pain point.

- **Redbox** disrupted Blockbuster Video by asking, "Why can't home video rental be more conveniently located closer to home?" At its peak, Blockbuster had over nine thousand stores around the world. As of March 31, 2019, just one store remains open.[15]
- **Netflix** disrupted cable TV by asking, "Why do commercials have to interrupt content?" Netflix now has 125 million subscribers worldwide.[16]
- **Dollar Shave Club** disrupted Gillette razors by asking, "Why are razor blades so expensive?" What started in 2012 as $1 razor blades in the founder's apartment complex was sold to Unilever in 2016 for $1 billion.[17]
- **Uber** disrupted the taxi industry by asking, "Why is licensing an expensive medallion necessary to transport people from place to place?" As a result, use of ride-hailing has skyrocketed. Across the United States, receipts from Certify software show that in Q1 2014, ride-hailing was a mere 8 percent of the business traveler ground transportation market, while rental cars were 55 percent and taxis were 37 percent. By Q1 2018, ride-hailing had grabbed 70.5 percent of the market, with rental cars getting 23.5 percent and taxis just 6 percent.[18] Usage of this service has expanded well beyond business travelers, and it's safe to assume that ride-hailing will continue to grow.

- **Amazon** has disrupted retail by asking, "Why does shopping have to be a physical destination?" They have redefined convenience. I was once in a marketing training where a participant said that Amazon helps her be a better mother. When her daughter forgets about the supplies she needs in a quick turnaround, Amazon comes to the rescue with two-day, next-day, or even two-hour delivery in some markets. While Amazon has given access to many brands that may not have otherwise had such a wide buying audience, the megapower has also disrupted retail, the shopping experience, and consumers' expectations of convenience. Quite simply, Amazon has been and continues to be a game-changer. Despite their impressive presence, Amazon continues to innovate, diversify, and try new approaches to maintain market share and drive loyalty.

A more recent example of disruptive innovation is Warby Parker, an online retailer of prescription glasses and sunglasses. A loyal customer, I appreciate the trendy variety of frames, excellent customer service, and the ability to try several frames at home before committing to purchase. To illustrate the origins of disruptive innovation, below is the imprinted message on the eyeglass cleaning cloth that comes inside of the complimentary glasses case:

Warby Parker in 100 Words
Once upon a time, a young man left his glasses on an airplane. He tried to buy new glasses. But new glasses were expensive. "Why is it so hard to buy stylish glasses without spending a fortune on them?" he wondered. He returned to school and told his friends. "We should start a company to sell amazing glasses for non-insane prices," said one. "We should make shopping for glasses fun," said another. "We should distribute a pair of glasses to someone in need for every pair sold," said a third. Eureka! Warby Parker was born.

EPILOGUE:
Thank you for reading "Warby Parker in 100 Words." You just read in less time than it takes to wash a dish, clean a smudge off your glasses, or consume six baby carrots at a responsible chewing pace. Not bad! 100 words goes by pretty fast. If you want more words, please visit warby parkers.com.[19]

Disruptive innovation is a parallel lesson on how to advance your career. Companies and organizations need to continue to evolve to stay ahead of the curve, or they risk losing relevance or, worse yet, their very existence. The same is true for you as you navigate your career. It doesn't matter how skilled you are, how many years of service you've accumulated, or how many times you've earned a good rating. Inevitably, there will be disruptors that require you to flex, evolve, or become obsolete.

Disruptors are emotional because they can disturb your peace, shake you out of your comfort zone, or change the power dynamics. In *Emotional Agility: Get Unstuck, Embrace Change and Thrive in Work and Life*, author Susan David discusses two common responses to dealing with negative emotions. "Bottlers" avoid negative emotions by pushing them to the side so they can get on with things and maintain an optimistic aura, lest they be thought of as weak. On the other hand, "brooders" get hooked on uncomfortable feelings, worrying and obsessing over feelings they can't let go of.[20]

On the other hand, David writes,

> Emotionally agile people are dynamic. They demonstrate flexibility in dealing with our fast-changing complex world. They are able to tolerate high levels of stress and endure setbacks, while remaining engaged, open and receptive. They understand that life isn't always easy, but they continue to act according to their most cherished values, and pursue their big, long-term goals. They still experience feelings of anger, sadness, and so on, but they face these with curiosity, self-compassion, and acceptance. And rather than letting these feelings derail them, emotionally agile people effectively turn themselves—warts and all—toward their loftiest ambitions.[21]

The following are a series of personal examples of how to navigate disruptions, external situations, and thinking that could be holding you back from achieving your potential.

NAVIGATING DISRUPTIONS

Meaning

I've experienced my share of disruptive situations in the workplace and in my personal life. My husband and I were college sweethearts and got married after graduation. But after nine months of marriage, we separated, and a few months later we divorced. It was a fairytale gone terribly wrong. While we were apart, we both did some serious reflection and soul-searching. I didn't realize it at the time, but emotional intelligence played a huge part in our healing process.

In addition to journaling, reflection, and prayer, I attended a transformative two and a half day workshop called Landmark Forum (https://www.landmarkworldwide.com/). There I learned so many powerful concepts that I still apply to this day. One of those concepts is about "meaning." For example, let's say it's the first day back from your vacation and your manager launches into a task-focused conversation without welcoming you back or asking if you enjoyed your time off. It's natural to draw conclusions: they don't care about me, they don't value me, or they are a terrible manager. However, each of those conclusions gives meaning, in your head, to what actually happened: you went into your manager's office, and they began discussing the business at hand.

Prior to learning this concept, I often added meaning to situations that happened with my then ex-husband. However, what I now realize is that we cause ourselves unnecessary torment when we add meaning to the facts. Stating the facts as if you are a third-party observer and re-sisting the urge to add meaning is one of many transformative concepts that was the beginning of a reconciliation.

Miraculously, we were remarried less than two years after being divorced. I wrote about it in my first book, *Love's Resurrection: A Spiritual Journey Through Marriage, Divorce, and Remarrying the Same Man*. We are still happily married as a family of five plus a dog. Despite the disruption, we are better and stronger for having pivoted and prioritized what was most important for us: family.

What meaning have you attached to situations?
How has that affected your words, actions, behaviors, and beliefs?

Mindset

My parents grew up in a once-segregated United States. As African Americans living in the "North," my mother began college in North Carolina in 1965, the year Jim Crow laws ended. She lasted only one year at the private school before transferring to a state school in Ohio. The restrictive rules were too oppressive for the independent lifestyle she was accustomed to. For example, she'd traveled on the city bus by herself to get allergy shots when she was only eight years old, but now at eighteen she was required to travel with a friend or chaperone on a bus downtown. Given the era of discrimination and heinous crimes committed against African Americans just because of the color of their skin, I can understand the college's perspective and rationale. Still, these and many other experiences shaped my parents' worldview.

One of the principles my parents taught me and often repeated, like so many other Black parents who grew up in the civil rights era, is that "you have to be twice as good to get half as far." In other words, even if you outwork others and contribute more than average, you'll never reach anywhere near the same level of success that others will. This lesson, coupled with the examples of my parents and so many other role models in my community, contributed to a strong work ethic. However, when I entered corporate America, after having attended predominately Black schools from primary through graduate school, it was difficult to assimilate into a new environment where I was truly a minority. The difficulty didn't stem from lack of ability; rather, it was my lack of exposure and a mindset from childhood that didn't serve me well.

One might conclude that I should have gone to a more diverse college for undergrad or graduate school; however, I don't regret my choice of education. Historically Black colleges and universities (HBCUs) offer a rich education inside and outside of the classroom whose benefits last a lifetime. In a survey by Pacesetters Unlimited, 87 percent of HBCU alumni say that their life is better because they attended an HBCU; 85 percent have a stronger network, and 59 percent believe that being an HBCU graduate has been an advantage in their career, in comparison to peers who did not attend an HBCU. Like the 94 percent of survey respondents who would still choose an HBCU if they had to turn back the clock and choose a college or university again, I share that perspective.[22]

My first manager in corporate America was amazing. He was smart, kind, and widely respected across Procter & Gamble. For context, he was also a White male. About a year after starting my job, I gave birth to a beautiful baby girl. My boss was supportive beyond belief, both personally and professionally. He gave me clothes that his toddlers had outgrown and an almost-new car seat. I was stunned by his generosity. I quickly realized that the mantra my parents instilled in me was not congruent with my beliefs as an adult, nor was it beneficial in the corporate environment. I am proud of my ethnic and cultural heritage; however, I had an epiphany, again at the Landmark Forum, that I'm more human than I am African American. I'm more human than I am woman. I'm more human than any label or title you can attach to me. This humanity is what allows me to engage with people with less pretense and judgment.

I don't fault or judge my parents for teaching me what they did; they made the best decision they could, based on their personal experiences and the information at their disposal. However, I decided to choose my beliefs instead of continuing to operate by default. My career blossomed at P&G, and I developed a wider, more diverse circle of friends. Had I not made this mindset tweak, there is no way I would have considered moving to a 10,000-person town in Central Pennsylvania with a 3 percent African American population, let alone working and thriving there.

What narrative are you playing into? Where did it stem from? Is it serving you or hindering you? Winning the battle of your mind is more than half the battle. Consider reframing your language and tweaking your mindset to operate from a place of purpose and power. For example:

Instead of . . .	**Try . . .**
• This is too hard.	This may take some time and effort.
• It's good enough.	Is this really my best work?
• I can't make this any better.	I can always improve, so I'll keep trying.

What are your values and beliefs?
Are they serving you well, or would you benefit from an evolution in thinking?

Understand the Rules of the Game

A few years into my first corporate job, I welcomed a new employee who had successfully completed a summer internship and returned for a full-time assignment. Rich[23] was well-accomplished, with an undergraduate degree from my alma mater, Florida A&M University, and a Harvard MBA. Like every new hire, he was required to complete several rounds of behavioral interviews, perform successfully during the internship, and even complete a series of intellectual and competency assessments liken to standardized tests.

Rich was, and is, exceptionally bright, but when he arrived at the company to find out that everyone around him was just as smart and just as dedicated as he was and some even more so, it was a rude awakening. He used to be a big fish in a small pond; now he was a small fish in a much bigger, more competitive pond where the stakes were high. What got him to that point would not get him over the next hurdle, so he needed new skills to navigate his career.

Not only were new skills needed, I helped him to understand the rules of the "game." The company rated its employees—1, 2, or 3. About 10 percent of the employee population received the highest rating of 1, and between 5 and 10 percent received the lowest rating of 3. Those employees were eventually coached out of the function or organization. After excelling throughout his life, Rich was shocked to receive a 2 rating. I coached him and helped him to understand that he was "competing" in a company full of superstars. Other marketers graduated in the top of their class and passed the same "entrance exams" he did. Yet we were all force-ranked into a bell curve. He left the company after a year and went on to lead a diverse career working in multiple industries. Once he understood the rules of that game, he decided not to play, and I commend his courage to pivot. Whatever you choose, make an informed choice rooted in knowledge and personal empowerment.

Do you understand the spoken and unspoken rules about how your organization defines success?

Learning and Unlearning

I was hired at Cardinal Health largely based on my expertise in consumer packaged goods and my diverse experience in large and mid-sized corporations. Part of a small team of cross-functional team members was internally tapped and externally hired to lead an initiative that went from concept to launch in fifteen months. This was a huge feat for a single product, let alone 160-plus products across five product categories in a new customer channel that was less familiar to the company.

We had the support from the CEO and many executive leaders. We were also under tremendous time pressure to launch. Besides a sense of urgency, we were operating in a matrixed environment whose systems weren't set up to support this new market. To make matters more complicated, many employees were also new to the marketing function. This made the task more stressful since they had to learn and do at the same time. The result was long days and even longer nights working from home. Coming from other companies and industries where fifty to sixty hour weeks were the norm, I wrongly assumed it was accepted at my new company. I'm a natural achiever who is driven by nature and willing to do whatever it takes to accomplish the goal. However, I was oblivious to the impact my leadership was having on others until my manager brought it to my attention. I accepted the feedback and became more aware of the norms, habits, and practices of my new company's employees. I realized that other people weren't emailing at 11 p.m., so I stopped sending emails at night because it was out of the norm and may have inadvertently sent a message that I expected my team, or others, to also work after hours from home. The timeline and team competition didn't allow for a 40-hour work week, so I still worked from home. However, I turned off the instant message service and saved the emails in my draft folder so I could send them in the morning.

This was one of many intentional tweaks I made to unlearn what made me successful in other organizations and to learn and adapt to an organizational culture to increase my effectiveness. Since that time, my role has expanded twice. I've gone from leading a startup business to running one of the largest product portfolios in the company. It wasn't my doing alone; I've had some amazing managers, mentors, sponsors, advocates, and an executive coach who have helped me along the journey. I'm also coachable and willing to accept feedback because I'm committed to advancing my career and increasing my impact on the business, organization, and, most important, people.

Stanford psychologist Carol Dweck authored *Mindset*, which describes the difference between a "fixed" versus "growth" mindset. According to Dweck, when someone has a fixed mindset, they believe that their basic abilities, intelligence, and talents are fixed traits that cannot be changed. They think, "That's just the way I am. Take it or leave it." On the other hand, people with a growth mindset have an underlying belief that their learning and intelligence can grow with time, experience, learning, and effort. "In this mindset, the hand you're dealt is just the starting point for development. This growth mindset is based on the belief that your basic qualities are things you can cultivate through your efforts. Although people may differ in every which way—in their initial talents and aptitudes, interests, or temperaments—everyone can change and grow through application and experience."[24]

Studies show that these beliefs about change can have a profound effect on behavior. Children who believe their intelligence is fixed underperform in courses that they find difficult relative to those who believe they can improve their effective intelligence by working hard. After all, those who are open to change and believe they can do better—and that their efforts matter—have a sense of agency of their performance and rise to the challenge. Setbacks and failures don't keep them down, and they persevere, even when they're frustrated.

If you're committed to realizing your leadership potential and advancing your career, agility is critical. One thing that's constant in life—personally and professionally—is change. To navigate change and stay in the game requires agility. Often, this occurs in small tweaks, not revolutionary pivots. I call it a one-degree shift.

Why does a single degree matter? Let's just say you were driving across the United States in a straight line from San Francisco to Washington, D.C., with a distance of roughly three thousand miles. If you changed the direction of your car just one degree, you would end up forty-two miles away in Baltimore, Maryland.

Did you know that the average, moderately active person walks 7,500 steps a day? Over the course of a lifetime, that's the equivalent of 110,000 miles.[23] I encourage you to think about your career as a marathon, not a sprint. To go the distance, it may require a few one-degree shifts to accelerate your career and achieve your goals. I hope this book has given you some nuggets and actionable steps to help you reach your desired career destination.

EMOTIONAL INTELLIGENCE INSIGHTS

47. Conquer clear, confident communication.

"Even the most skilled expert loses credibility without communicating with clarity and conviction."

When you want to effectively persuade others, first understand the objective, decision makers, influencers, and barriers. This will help guide your content, whether written or verbal.

Although the STAR acronym is often used in interviews (situation, task, action, and result), it's an easy-to-apply, everyday framework that can help you communicate more confidently. STAR concisely describes what needs to be done, by whom, when, and the anticipated outcome.

48. Experience is the best teacher.

Research shows that only 10 percent of our development comes from formal training, while 20 percent comes from coaching and mentoring.

"70 percent of our development occurs on the job."

Regardless of your college education or training, technical competence—the what—is built by doing. This requires flexibility. The how is even more important and can be perfected through personal experience, direct observation, coaching from your manager, and advice from others. Being open to this feedback will help you avoid learning the hard way.

49. Leave room in your schedule.

Scheduling every hour of the day leaves no room for creativity, unexpected tasks, impromptu conversations, or thinking time. This can result in feeling frustrated and overwhelmed.

To create more capacity and avoid feeling overwhelmed, schedule meetings with yourself to accomplish specific tasks; block free time; and if allowed, work off-site or from home periodically to increase productivity.

"Some of the most effective relationships are nurtured through just-in-time dialogue and drive-by meetings."

50. Only handle it once (OHIO).

Email is a necessary tool in the workplace. However, when email becomes your to-do list, you can become a slave to the device and feel out of control, especially when there are competing demands and changing priorities.

"Use the OHIO method for email so you only handle it once."

Try following the 4-D (delete, do, delegate, delay) method to manage emotions and stress levels while minimizing your inbox:

- *Delete* junk email or previous versions of a long email string.
- Take immediate action on emails that require you to *do* something, then file or delete the email.
- *Delegate* responsibility by replying or forwarding the email to the person who needs to act.
- If the email requires your attention and you decide to *delay* action, create a calendar invite for yourself, file it in an electronic task list, or write down the task on a separate to-do list. File the email using a logical, easy-to-remember system so you revisit the email when it's time to act and avoid reading the inbox email twice.

51. Act confident until you feel confident.

Most careers don't come with a playbook of how-to directions. It's more likely that you'll be faced with unfamiliar situations to figure out along the way.

"Vulnerability is an important part of growth."

It's okay to admit, "I don't know, but we'll figure it out together." That's humble confidence. Believe in your heart that you are capable, and partner with other great minds to develop a solution that builds both competence and confidence.

52. Prosper where you're planted.

As you progress in your career, getting promoted to the next level may lose its appeal. Sometimes there are other factors—personal and professional—that become more important than upward mobility. Whether you're seeking a lateral assignment that offers new challenges or you're committed to mastering your current role, always remember that doing your current job with excellence is the first step to a fruitful career. Stay closely in tune with your emotions, the drivers, and their impact on you.

"Above all, guard against complacency—it's the enemy of being."

Quick Reference Guide

52 Insights across Twelve Emotional Intelligence Competencies

SELF-AWARENESS

Emotional Self-Awareness

1. Know thyself.
4. Instability reflects poorly on your capabilities.
5. Perception is reality.
7. The common denominator might be you.
15. Forgive frequently.
30. Control the "controllables."
33. Be consistent.
41. Leaders are deeply human and, therefore, deeply imperfect.
42. Agility is about making tweaks without sacrificing authenticity.
43. Leadership can be lonely.
45. Self-worth is not defined by your job or your boss.
46. The fit isn't always mutual.
48. Experience is the best teacher.
49. Leave room in your schedule.
50. Only handle it once.
51. Act confident until you feel confident.
52. Prosper where you're planted.

SELF-MANAGEMENT

Emotional Self-Control

2. Bring your whole self to work, but be selective with what you share.
6. Feedback is a gift that others don't have to give.
15. Forgive frequently.
20. Consider the trade-offs.
21. Be patient for growth.
30. Control the "controllables."
33. Be consistent.
39. Peers aren't your competition.
41. Leaders are deeply human and, therefore, deeply imperfect.
42. Agility is about making tweaks without sacrificing authenticity.
43. Leadership can be lonely.
50. Only handle it once.

Achievement Orientation

7. The common denominator might be you.
8. Quantify your impact, not your activities.
10. I'm ready for the next level. Now what?
16. Leadership is about learning as well as unlearning.
21. Be patient for growth.
23. Give your employees plenty of airtime.
26. Selling ideas without sharing potential downsides diminishes your credibility.
29. Why meet before the meeting?

Positive Outlook

6. Feedback is a gift that others don't have to give.
10. I'm ready for the next level. Now what?
16. Leadership is about learning as well as unlearning.
21. Be patient for growth.
25. Facts tell, but stories sell.
27. It's natural to be passionate about your idea, but often passion is not enough.

41. Leaders are deeply human and, therefore, deeply imperfect.
45. Self-worth is not defined by your job or your boss.
51. Act confident until you feel confident.

Adaptability

  4. Instability reflects poorly on your capabilities.
  5. Perception is reality.
  7. The common denominator might be you.
10. I'm ready for the next level. Now what?
16. Leadership is about learning as well as unlearning.
27. It's natural to be passionate about your idea, but often passion is not enough.
30. Control the "controllables."
31. Every organization has its own DNA.
34. People first, titles second.
42. Agility is about making tweaks without sacrificing authenticity.
48. Experience is the best teacher.
50. Only handle it once.

SOCIAL AWARENESS

Empathy

  4. Instability reflects poorly on your capabilities.
  5. Perception is reality.
  6. Feedback is a gift that others don't have to give.
  7. The common denominator might be you.
11. Understand their mindset, motivations, and fears.
12. Strive to make your manager look good.
14. Extend grace.
17. Call people by name.
22. Hire for character, not just competence.
32. Diversify your network.
34. People first, titles second.
35. Maximize informal communication.
36. Share your weekend highlight reel.

37. If it doesn't fit, don't force it.
40. Who you marry . . . matters.

Organizational Awareness

9. Say *yes* to the invite.
11. Understand their mindset, motivations, and fears.
13. Some situations are above your paygrade.
20. Consider the trade-offs.
28. Incentives drive behavior.
29. Why meet before the meeting?
31. Every organization has its own DNA.
44. Friends and "work friends" are not synonymous.
46. The fit isn't always mutual.

RELATIONSHIP MANAGEMENT

Influence

9. Say *yes* to the invite.
10. I'm ready for the next level. Now what?
11. Understand their mindset, motivations, and fears.
12. Strive to make your manager look good.
18. Culture reigns supreme.
19. Clarity and accountability drive results.
20. Consider the trade-offs.
23. Give your employees plenty of airtime.
25. Facts tell, but stories sell.
26. Selling ideas without sharing potential downsides diminishes your credibility.
28. Incentives drive behavior.
29. Why meet before the meeting?
34. People first, titles second.
38. You don't have all the answers.
39. Peers aren't your competition.
47. Conquer clear, confident communication.

Coach and Mentor

10. I'm ready for the next level. Now what?
23. Give your employees plenty of airtime.
24. Slow to hire, swift to fire.
35. Maximize informal communication.
38. You don't have all the answers.

Conflict Management

12. Strive to make your manager look good.
14. Extend grace.
15. Forgive frequently.
20. Consider the trade-offs.
24. Slow to hire, swift to fire.
29. Why meet before the meeting?
40. Who you marry . . . matters.

Inspirational Leadership

10. I'm ready for the next level. Now what?
18. Culture reigns supreme.
19. Clarity and accountability drive results.
23. Give your employees plenty of airtime.
25. Facts tell, but stories sell.
27. It's natural to be passionate about your idea, but often passion is not enough.
38. You don't have all the answers.

Teamwork

8. Quantify your impact, not your activities.
14. Extend grace.
15. Forgive frequently.
17. Call people by name.
18. Culture reigns supreme.
19. Clarity and accountability drive results.
20. Consider the trade-offs.
23. Give your employees plenty of airtime.

27. It's natural to be passionate about your idea, but often passion is not enough.
29. Why meet before the meeting?
32. Diversify your network.
34. People first, titles second.
35. Maximize informal communication.
39. Peers aren't your competition.
44. Friends and "work friends" are not synonymous.
49. Leave room in your schedule.
51. Act confident until you feel confident.

Notes

INTRODUCTION

1. "Emotional Quotient (EQ) and IQ," Free Management eBooks, accessed July 26, 2018, http://www.free-management-ebooks.com/faqpp/understanding -03.htm.
2. "Emotional and Social Intelligence Competencies: An Overview," Key Step Media, last modified April 11, 2017, https://www.keystepmedia.com /emotional-social-intelligence-leadership-competencies/.

CHAPTER 1

1. "About Us. Coca-Cola History," The Coca-Cola Company, https:// www.worldofcoca-cola.com/about-us/coca-cola-history/, accessed November 1, 2018.
2. "Coca-Cola Local Flavors," The Coca-Cola Company, https://us.coca -cola.com/coca-cola-local-flavors/, accessed November 1, 2018.
3. Fred Barbash and Travis M. Andrews, "'I'd Like to Buy the World a Coke': The Story Behind the World's Most Famous Ad, in Memoriam Its Creator," *Washington Post,* May 17, 2016, https://www.washingtonpost. com/news/morning-mix/wp/2016/05/17/id-like-to-buy-the-world-a-coke -the-story-behind-the-worlds-most-famous-ad-whose-creator-has-died-at -89/?noredirect=on&utm_term=.ec3a24dd3592.
4. Barbash and Andrews, "'I'd Like to Buy the World a Coke.'"
5. Joe Lynch, "'Mad Men' Finale: The Real Story Behind the Coke Jingle That Became a Billboard Hit," *Billboard,* May 18, 2015, https://www.billboard .com/articles/news/6568774/mad-men-finale-buy-the-world-a-coke-song.

6. "Who We Are," The Coca-Cola Company, https://www.coca-colacom pany.com/careers/who-we-are-infographic, accessed November 1, 2018.

7. "Who We Are."

8. Mary Fernandez, "32 of the BEST Value Propositions (Plus How to Write Your Own)," OptinMonster, https://optinmonster.com/32-value-prop ositions-that-are-impossible-to-resist/, last modified January 7, 2019.

9. "One Assessment to Discover the One True You," Gallup Strengths Center, accessed November 1, 2018, https://www.gallupstrengthscenter.com /home/en-us/cliftonstrengths-how-it-works.

10. "What Is the Difference Between a Talent and a Strength?" Clifton-Strengths® for Students, accessed November 1, 2018, http://www.strengths quest.com/help/general/143096/difference-talent-strength.aspx.

11. "A FAQ Guide to Strengths at Rollins," Rollins College, Florida, ac-cessed November 1, 2018, https://www.rollins.edu/student-affairs/images-docs /faq-guide-strengths.pdf.

12. "StrengthsFinder Domains—4 Areas of Strength," Strengths Coaching & Training, accessed November 1, 2018, https://strengthscoachingandtraining .com/strengthsfinder-clifton-strengths-assessment/strengthsfinder-domains -categories/.

CHAPTER 2

1. "Equilar | Associated Press CEO Pay Study 2018," Equilar, May 24, 2018, https://www.equilar.com/reports/57-equilar-associated-press-ceo-pay -study-2018.html.

2. "Mental Illness," National Institute of Mental Health, last modified Feb-ruary 2019, http://www.nimh.nih.gov/health/statistics/prevalence/any-mental -illness-ami-among-adults.shtml.

3. "Mental Health Facts in America," National Alliance on Mental Illness, accessed December 31, 2018, https://www.nami.org/NAMI/media/NAMI -Media/Infographics/GeneralMHFacts.pdf.

4. Melissa Healy, "For Those in Posh Jobs, Depression May Be Harder to Treat," *Los Angeles Times*, September 21, 2016, https://www.latimes.com/sci ence/sciencenow/la-sci-sn-job-status-depression-20160921-snap-story.html.

5. Healy, "For Those in Posh Jobs."

6. Healy, "For Those in Posh Jobs."

7. Healy, "For Those in Posh Jobs."

8. Alina S. Williams, "Workplace Stress," Psych Central, last modified Oc-tober 8, 2018, https://psychcentral.com/lib/workplace-stress/.

9. "Innovation Matters. New Innovation Research," PA Consulting, accessed December 31, 2018, http://www2.paconsulting.com/rs/526-hze-833 images/innovation-matters-report.pdf.

10. Richard Fry, "Millennials Are the Largest Generation in the U.S. Labor Force," Pew Research Center, April 11, 2018, https://www.pewresearch .org/fact-tank/2018/04/11/millennials-largest-generation-us-labor-force/.

CHAPTER 3

1. "Johnson & Johnson Credo," Johnson & Johnson, accessed December 23, 2018, https://www.jnj.com/credo.

2. "Johnson & Johnson Credo."

3. George Ella Lyon, "Where I'm From," George Ella Lyon: Writer & Teacher, accessed December 23, 2018, http://www.georgeellalyon.com/where .html.

CHAPTER 4

1. "Women in the Workplace 2016," LeanIn.org and McKinsey & Company, September 2016, http://www.mckinsey.com/business-functions/organi zation/our-insights/women-in-the-workplace-2016.

2. *Merriam-Webster Online*, s. v. "influence," accessed December 20, 2018, https://www.merriam-webster.com/dictionary/influence.

3. *Merriam-Webster Online*, s. v. "office politics," accessed December 20, 2018, https://www.merriam-webster.com/dictionary/officepolitics.

4. Kathryn Heath, Jill Flynn, Mary Davis Holt, and Diana Faison, *The Influence Effect: A New Path to Power for Women Leaders* (San Francisco: Berrett-Koehler Publishers, 2017), 4.

CHAPTER 5

1. Carl Rogers, "Accurate Empathic Understanding," accessed December 31, 2018, https://www.centerfortheperson.org/pdf/accurate-empathic-under standing.pdf.

2. Helen Riess and Liz Neporent, *The Empathy Effect: 7 Neuroscience-Based Keys to Transforming the Way We Live, Love, Work and Connect Across Differences* (Boulder: Sounds True, 2018), 10.

3. Richard Boyatzis and Annie McKee, *Resonant Leadership: Renewing Yourself and Connecting with Others Through Mindfulness, Hope and Compassion* (Boston: Harvard Business Review Press, 2005), 160–62.

4. Belinda Parmar, "The Most Empathetic Companies, 2016," *Harvard Business Review*, last modified December 20, 2016, https://hbr.org/2016/12/the-most-and-least-empathetic-companies-2016#.

5. Daniel Goleman and Richard Boyatzis, "Social Intelligence and the Biology of Leadership," *Harvard Business Review*, September 2008, http://files-au.clickdimensions.com/aisnsweduau-akudz/files/inteligencia-social-y-biologia-de-un-lider.pdf.

6. Goleman and Boyatzis, "Social Intelligence and the Biology of Leadership."

7. Riess and Neporent, *The Empathy Effect*, 149.

8. Piercarlo Valdesolo, Jennifer Ouyang, and David DeSteno, "The Rhythm of Joint Action: Synchrony Promotes Cooperative Ability." *Journal of Experimental Social Psychology* 46, no. 4 (July 2010): 693–95, https://www.sciencedirect.com/science/article/pii/S0022103110000430?via%3Dihub.

9. Goleman and Boyatzis, "Social Intelligence and the Biology of Leadership."

10. Riess and Neporent, *The Empathy Effect*, 3–4.

11. "Communication Model by Albert Mehrabian," Toolshero, accessed August 25, 2019, https://www.toolshero.com/communication-skills/communication-model-mehrabian/.

12. Albert Mehrabian, *Nonverbal Communication* (Chicago: Aldine-Atherton, 1972), 182.

13. "Prosody," *Wikipedia*, accessed December 31, 2018, https://en.wikipedia.org/wiki/Prosody_(linguistics).

14. Jean Decety and Philip Jackson, "The Functional Architecture of Human Empathy," *Behavioral and Cognitive Neuroscience Reviews* 3, no. 2 (June 2004): 71–100.

15. Simone Shamay-Tsoory, Judith Aharon-Peretz, and Danielle Perry, "Two Systems for Empathy: A Double Dissociation Between Emotional and Cognitive Empathy in Inferior Frontal Gyrus Versus Ventromedial Prefrontal Lesions," *Brain: A Journal of Neurology* 132 (Pt 3) (March 2009): 617–27, http://doi.org/10.1093/brain/awn279.

16. Tania Singer and Claus Lamm, "The Social Neuroscience of Empathy," *Annals of the New York Academy of Sciences* 1156 (March 2009): 85, http://doi.org/10.1111/j.1749-6632.2009.04418.x.

17. Richard Fry, "Millennials Are the Largest Generation in the U.S. Labor Force," Pew Research Center, April 11, 2018, https://www.pewresearch.org /fact-tank/2018/04/11/millennials-largest-generation-us-labor-force/.

18. "Time Inc. Study Reveals That 'Digital Natives' Switch Between Devices and Platforms Every Two Minutes, Use Media to Regulate Their Mood," Business Wire, April 9, 2012, https://www.businesswire.com/news /home/20120409005536/en/Time-Study-Reveals-%E2%80%9CDigital -Natives%E2%80%9D-Switch-Devices.

19. Brian Steinberg, "Study: Young Consumers Switch Media 27 Times an Hour," *Ad Age*, April 9, 2012, https://adage.com/article/news/study-young -consumers-switch-media-27-times-hour/234008/.

20. Jeffrey Cole, Michael Suman, Phoebe Schramm, and Liuning Zhou, "The 2017 Digital Future Report," *University of Southern California Annenberg*, last modified 2017, http://www.digitalcenter.org/wp-content /uploads/2013/10/2017-Digital-Future-Report.pdf.

21. Cole, Suman, Schramm, and Zhou, "The 2017 Digital Future Report."

22. Cole, Suman, Schramm, and Zhou, "The 2017 Digital Future Report."

23. SWNS, "Americans Check Their Phones 80 Times a Day: Study," *New York Post*, November 8, 2017, https://nypost.com/2017/11/08/americans -check-their-phones-80-times-a-day-study/.

24. Quentin Fottrell, "People Spend Most of Their Waking Hours Staring at Screens." *Market Watch*, August 4, 2018, https://www.market watch.com/story/people-are-spending-most-of-their-waking-hours-staring-at -screens-2018-08-01.

25. Fottrell, "People Spend Most of Their Waking Hours Staring at Screens."

26. "Understanding Addiction," Help Guide, accessed March 23, 2019, https://www.helpguide.org/harvard/how-addiction-hijacks-the-brain.htm.

27. Jon Simpson and Forbes Agency Council, "Finding Brand Success in the Digital World," *Forbes*, August 25, 2017, https://www.forbes.com /sites/forbesagencycouncil/2017/08/25/finding-brand-success-in-the-digital -world/#39a16aeb626e.

28. Kent C. Berridge and Terry E. Robinson, "What Is the Role of Dopamine in Reward: Hedonic Impact, Reward Learning, or Incentive Salience?" *Brain Research Reviews* 28, no. 3 (December 1998): 309–69, https://lsa.umich.edu/psych/research&labs/berridge/publications/Berridge &RobinsonBrResRev1998.pdf.

29. Andrew Przybylski and Netta Weinstein, "Can You Connect with Me Now? How the Presence of Mobile Communication Technology Influences Face-to-Face Conversation Quality," *Journal of Social and Personal Relationships Research* 303, no. 3 (2012): 237–46, https://journals.sagepub.com/doi /pdf/10.1177/0265407512453827.

30. Lara Srivastava, "Mobile Phones and the Evolution of Social Behavior," *Behaviour & Information Technology* 24, no. 2 (2005): 111–29, accessed March 23, 2019, http://doi.org/10.1080/01449290512331321910.

31. Srivastava, "Mobile Phones and the Evolution of Social Behavior."

32. Riess and Neporent, *The Empathy Effect*, 118.

CHAPTER 6

1. George Bonanno, Maren Westphal, and Anthony Mancini, "Resilience to Loss and Potential Trauma," *Annual Review of Clinical Psychology* 7, no. 1 (April 2010): 511–35.

2. Rich Fernandez, "5 Ways to Boost Your Resilience at Work," *Harvard Business Review*, June 27, 2016, https://hbr.org/2016/06/627-building-resil ience-ic-5-ways-to-build-your-personal-resilience-at-work.

3. Fernandez, "5 Ways to Boost Your Resilience at Work."

4. Fernandez, "5 Ways to Boost Your Resilience at Work."

5. Fernandez, "5 Ways to Boost Your Resilience at Work."

6. Fernandez, "5 Ways to Boost Your Resilience at Work."

7. Carol P. Kaplan, Sandra Turner, Elaine Norman, and Kathy Stillson, "Promoting Resilience Strategies: A Modified Consultation Model," *Children & Schools* 18, no. 3 (July 1996): 158–68, https://doi.org/10.1093/cs/18.3.158.

8. Ellen Van Velsor and Leslie Jean Brittain, "Why Executives Derail: Perspectives across Time and Cultures," *The Academy of Management Execu-tive (1993-2005)* 9, no. 4 (1995): 62–72, http://www.jstor.org/stable/4165289.

9. Derek Roger, Nick Petrie, and the Center for Creative Leadership, *Work Without Stress: Building a Resilient Mindset for Lasting Success* (New York: McGraw-Hill Education, 2017), 5.

10. Michele M. Tugade and Barbara L. Fredrickson, "Resilient Individuals Use Positive Emotions to Bounce Back from Negative Emotional Experi-ences," *Journal of Personality and Social Psychology* 86, no. 2 (2004): 320–33.

11. "Stress . . . at Work," Centers for Disease Control and Prevention: The National Institute for Occupational Safety and Health, DHHS (NIOSH) Publication Number 99-101 (1999), https://www.cdc.gov/niosh/docs/99-101/.

12. "5 Key Questions about Employee Resilience," BetterUp, accessed June 1, 2019. https://get.betterup.co/rs/600-WTC-654/images/BetterUp-5-key -question-about-employee-resilience.pdf.

13. "5 Key Questions about Employee Resilience."

14. Zelana Montminy, *21 Days to Resilience: How to Transcend the Daily Grind, Deal with the Tough Stuff, and Discover Your Strongest Self* (New York: Harper Collins, 2016), 4.

15. Roger, Petrie, and the Center for Creative Leadership, *Work Without Stress*, inside cover.

16. Ann Masten and Dante Cicchetti, "Risk and Resilience in Development and Psychopathology: The Legacy of Norman Garmezy," *Development and Psychopathology* [Special section] 24, 333–34 (2012).

17. Barbara Fredrickson, Michele Tugade, Christian E. Waugh, and Gregory R. Larkin, "What Good Are Positive Emotions in Crises? A Prospective Study of Resilience and Emotions Following the Terrorist Attacks on the United States on September 11, 2001," *Journal of Personality and Social Psychology* 84, no. 2 (February 2003): 365–76.

18. Fredrickson et al., "What Good Are Positive Emotions in Crises?"

19. Judith Herman, *Trauma and Recovery: The Aftermath of Violence from Domestic Abuse to Political Terror* (New York: Basic Books, 1992), 33.

20. Herman, *Trauma and Recovery*, 33.

21. Amy Guntry, Patricia Frazier, Howard Tennen, Patricia Tomich, Ty Tashiro, and Crystal Park, "Moderators of the Relation between Perceived and Actual Posttraumatic Growth," *Psychological Trauma: Theory, Research, Practice and Policy* 3 (2011): 61–66.

22. David Feldman and Lee Daniel Kravetz, *Supersurvivors: The Surprising Link Between Suffering and Success* (New York: Harper Collins Publishers, 2014), inside cover.

23. Julia Kim-Cohen et al., "Genetic and Environmental Processes in Young Children's Resilience and Vulnerability to Socioeconomic Deprivation," *Child Development* 75, no. 3 (2004): 651–68.

24. Fredrickson et al., "What Good Are Positive Emotions in Crises?"

25. Fredrickson et al., "What Good Are Positive Emotions in Crises?"

26. Diane L. Contu, "How Resilience Works," *Harvard Business Review*, May 2002, https://hbr.org/2002/05/how-resilience-works.

27. Montminy, *21 Days to Resilience*, 123.

28. Gregory E. Miller and Carsten Wrosch. "You've Gotta Know When to Fold 'Em: Goal Disengagement and Systemic Inflammation in Adolescence." *Psychological Science* 18, no. 9 (September 2007): 773–77. doi:10.1111/j.1467 -9280.2007.01977.x.

29. Carsten Wrosch, Michael Scheier, Charles Carver, and Richard Schult. "The Importance of Goal Disengagement in Adaptive Self-Regulation: When Giving Up Is Beneficial," *Self and Identity* 2, no. 1 (2003): 1–20.

30. Feldman and Kravetz, *Supersurvivors*, 25–26.

31. Feldman and Kravetz, *Supersurvivors*, 27–28.

32. Jay Jackman and Myra Strober, "Fear of Feedback," *Harvard Business Review*, April 2003, https://hbr.org/2003/04/fear-of-feedback.

33. Rasmus Hougaad, Jacqueline Cater, and Gitte Dybkjaer, "Spending 10 Minutes a Day on Mindfulness Subtly Changes the Way You React to Ev-

erything, *Harvard Business Review*, January 18, 2017, https://hbr.org/2017/01/spending-10-minutes-a-day-on-mindfulness-subtly-changes-the-way-you-react-to-everything.

34. Linda Graham, *Bouncing Back: Rewiring Your Brain for Maximum Resilience and Well-Being* (Novato, CA: New World Library, 2013), 307.

35. "What Is Diaphragmatic Breathing?" Healthline, accessed June 2, 2019, https://www.healthline.com/health/diaphragmatic-breathing.

36. Michele Tugade, Barbara Fredrickson, and Lisa Feldman Barrett, "Psychological Resilience and Positive Emotional Granularity: Examining the Benefits of Positive Emotions on Coping and Health," *Journal of Personality* 72, no. 6 (December 2004): 1161–90.

37. Matthew Lieberman, Naomi Eisenberger, Molly J. Crockett, Sabrina M. Tom, Jennifer H. Pfeifer, and Baldwin M. Way, "Putting Feelings into Words," *Psychological Science* 18, no. 5 (2007): 421–28, https://doi.org/10.1111/j.1467-9280.2007.01916.x.

38. Scott Mautz, "Super-Resilient People Are 6 Times More Likely to Do This 1 Thing, According to New Research," *Inc. Magazine*, May 7, 2019, https://www.inc.com/scott-mautz/super-resilient-people-are-6-times-more-likely-to-do-this-1-thing-according-to-new-research.html.

39. Mautz, "Super-Resilient People."

40. Viktor Emil Frankl, *Man's Search for Meaning: An Introduction to Logotherapy* (New York: Simon & Schuster, 1984), 116.

41. Laura Yamhure Thompson, C. R. Snyder, Lesa Hoffman, Scott T. Michael, Heather N. Rasmussen, Laura S. Billings, and Danae E. Roberts, "Dispositional Forgiveness of Self, Others and Situations," *Journal of Personality* 73 (2005): 313–59.

42. Thompson et al., "Dispositional Forgiveness of Self, Others and Situations."

43. Loren L. Toussaint, David R. Williams, Marc A. Musick, and Susan A. Everson-Rose, "Why Forgiveness May Protect against Depression: Hopelessness as an Explanatory Mechanism," *Personality and Mental Health 2* (2008): 89–103.

44. Toussaint et al. "Why Forgiveness May Protect against Depression."

45. Toussaint et al. "Why Forgiveness May Protect against Depression."

46. Kenneth I. Pargament, Bruce W. Smith, Harold G. Koenig, and Lisa Perez. "Patterns of Positive and Negative Religious Coping with Major Life Stressors," *Journal for the Scientific Study of Religion* 37 (1998): 710–24.

47. Mautz, "Super-Resilient People."

48. Feldman and Kravetz, *Supersurvivors*, 50.

CHAPTER 7

1. Eudie Pak, "Walt Disney's Rocky Road to Success," February 21, 2019, https://www.biography.com/news/walt-disney-failures.

2. "Milton Hershey Biography," Biography.com, accessed June 29, 2019, https://www.biography.com/business-figure/milton-hershey.

3. "Milton Hershey School FAQs," Milton Hershey School, accessed June 29, 2019, https://www.mhskids.org/about/faq-2/.

4. John Greathouse, "7 Lessons from the Beatles' Biggest Failure," *Inc. Magazine*, February 6, 2013, https://www.inc.com/john-greathouse/7-lessons-from-the-beatles-biggest-failure.html.

5. John MacMillan, "Awards and Achievements," Rockapedia, October 14, 2014, http://www.rockapedia.com/biography/the-beatles/awards-and-achievements.

6. Jeff Stibel, "Lady Gaga: A Profile in Failure," May 27, 2015, https://www.linkedin.com/pulse/lady-gaga-profile-failure-jeff-stibel/.

7. Elizabeth Andal, "10 Famous Failures to Success Stories That Will Inspire You to Carry On," Lifehack, last modified May 14, 2019, https://www.lifehack.org/articles/communication/10-famous-failures-that-will-inspire-you-success.html.

8. Elizabeth Andal, "10 Famous Failures."

9. Jeff Stibel, "Oprah Winfrey: A Profile in Failure," December 5, 2014, https://www.linkedin.com/pulse/20141205173028-461078-oprah-winfrey-a-profile-in-failure/.

10. Banji Ganchrow, "Oprah Winfrey's Greatest Accomplishments," Longevity, 2015, https://longevity.media/oprah-winfreys-greatest-accomplishments.

11. Mark Murphy, "Neuroscience Explains Why You Need to Write Down Your Goals If You Actually Want to Achieve Them," *Forbes*, April 15, 2018, http://www.forbes.com/sites/markmurphy/2018/04/15/neuroscience-explains-why-you-need-to-write-down-your-goals-if-you-actually-want-to-achieve-them/.

12. Richard Fry, "Millennials Are the Largest Generation in the U.S. Labor Force," Pew Research Center, April 11, 2018, https://www.pewresearch.org/fact-tank/2018/04/11/millennials-largest-generation-us-labor-force/.

13. "Disruptive Innovation," Clayton Christensen.com, accessed December 19, 2019, http://claytonchristensen.com/key-concepts/.

14. Marc Emmer, "95 Percent of New Products Fail. Here Are 6 Steps to Make Sure Yours Don't," *Inc. Magazine*, July 6, 2018, https://www.inc.com/marc-emmer/95-percent-of-new-products-fail-here-are-6-steps-to-make-sure-yours-dont.html.

15. "Blockbuster LLC," *Wikipedia*, accessed July 1, 2019, https://en.wikipedia.org/wiki/Blockbuster_LLC.

16. Arne Alsin, "The Future of Media: Disruptions, Revolutions and the Quest for Distribution," *Forbes*, July 19, 2018, https://www.forbes.com/sites/aalsin/2018/07/19/the-future-of-media-disruptions-revolutions-and-the-quest-for-distribution/.

17. "Unilever Buys Dollar Shave Club, Co-Founder Michael Dubin to Remain CEO," CNBC, July 20, 2016, accessed July 1, 2019, https://www.cnbc.com/2016/07/20/unilever-buys-dollar-shave-club-co-founder-michael-dubin-to-remain-ceo.html.

18. Michael Goldstein, "Dislocation and Its Discontents: Ride-Sharing's Impact on the Taxi Industry," *Forbes*, June 8, 2018, https://www.forbes.com/sites/michaelgoldstein/2018/06/08/uber-lyft-taxi-drivers/#514e3c8859f0.

19. Alli McKee, "[Your Company] in 100 Words: How Warby Parker Uses Product to Make Their Story Stick," Medium, November 1, 2017, https://medium.com/show-and-sell/your-company-in-100-words-e7558b0b1077.

20. Susan David, *Emotional Agility: Get Unstuck, Embrace Change, and Thrive in Work and Life* (New York: Avery, an imprint of Penguin Random House, 2016), 43–62.

21. Susan David, *Emotional Agility*, 6.

22. "Pacesetters Unlimited Online Survey among HBCU Alumni," Pacesetters Unlimited, 2016, http://pacesettersunlimited.org/hbcu.html.

23. Name has been changed to protect confidentiality.

24. Carol Dweck, *Mindset* (New York: Ballantine Books, 2006), 6–7.

25. "Brain Post: How Far Does the Average Human Walk in a Lifetime?" Snow Brains, June 20, 2018, https://snowbrains.com/brain-post-how-far-does-the-average-human-walk-in-a-lifetime/.

Bibliography

Alsin, Arne. "The Future of Media: Disruptions, Revolutions and the Quest for Distribution." *Forbes*, July 19, 2018. https://www.forbes.com/sites/aalsin/2018/07/19/the-future-of-media-disruptions-revolutions-and-the-quest-for-distribution/.

Andal, Elizabeth. "10 Famous Failures to Success Stories That Will Inspire You to Carry On." Lifehack. Last modified May 14, 2019. https://www.lifehack.org/articles/communication/10-famous-failures-that-will-inspire-you-success.html.

Barbash, Fred, and Andrews, Travis M. "'I'd Like to Buy the World a Coke': The Story Behind the World's Most Famous Ad, in Memoriam Its Creator." *Washington Post*, May 17, 2016. https://www.washingtonpost.com/news/morning-mix/wp/2016/05/17/id-like-to-buy-the-world-a-coke-the-story-behind-the-worlds-most-famous-ad-whose-creator-has-died-at-89/?noredirect=on&utm_term=.ec3a24dd3592.

Berridge, Kent C., and Terry E. Robinson. "What Is the Role of Dopamine in Reward: Hedonic Impact, Reward Learning, or Incentive Salience?" *Brain Research Reviews* 28, no. 3 (December 1998): 309–69. https://lsa.umich.edu/psych/research&labs/berridge/publications/Berridge&RobinsonBrResRev1998.pdf.

BetterUp. "5 Key Questions about Employee Resilience." Accessed June 1, 2019. https://get.betterup.co/rs/600-WTC-654/images/BetterUp-5-key-question-about-employee-resilience.pdf.

Biography.com. "Milton Hershey Biography." Accessed June 29, 2019. https://www.biography.com/business-figure/milton-hershey.

Bonanno, George, Maren Westphal, and Anthony Mancini. "Resilience to Loss and Potential Trauma." *Annual Review of Clinical Psychology* 7, no. 1 (April 2010): 511–35.

Boyatzis, Richard, and Annie McKee. *Resonant Leadership: Renewing Yourself and Connecting with Others Through Mindfulness, Hope and Compassion.* Boston: Harvard Business Review Press, 2005.

Business Wire. "Time Inc. Study Reveals That 'Digital Natives' Switch Between Devices and Platforms Every Two Minutes, Use Media to Regulate Their Mood." April 9, 2012. https://www.businesswire.com/news/home/20120409005536/en/Time-Study-Reveals-%E2%80%9CDigital-Natives%E2%80%9D-Switch-Devices.

Center for Disease Control and Prevention. "Stress . . . at Work." The National Institute for Occupational Safety and Health: DHHS (NIOSH) Publication Number 99-101 (1999). https://www.cdc.gov/niosh/docs/99-101/.

Chang, Olivia. "Coca-Cola Is Replacing Coke Zero with a New Drink." CNN Money, July 26. 2017. https://money.cnn.com/2017/07/26/news/companies/coke-zero/index.html.

CliftonStrengths® for Students. "What Is the Difference Between a Talent and a Strength?" Accessed November 1, 2018. http://www.strengthsquest.com/help/general/143096/difference-talent-strength.aspx.

CNBC. "Unilever Buys Dollar Shave Club, Co-Founder Michael Dubin to remain CEO." July 20, 2016. https://www.forbes.com/sites/aalsin/2018/07/19/the-future-of-media-disruptions-revolutions-and-the-quest-for-distribution/.

Coca-Cola Company. "About Us. Coca-Cola History." Accessed November 1, 2018. https://www.worldofcoca-cola.com/about-us/coca-cola-history/.

Coca-Cola Company. "Coca-Cola Local Flavors." Accessed November 1, 2018. https://us.coca-cola.com/coca-cola-local-flavors/.

Coca-Cola Company. "Who We Are." Accessed November 1, 2018. https://www.coca-colacompany.com/careers/who-we-are-infographic.

Cole, Jeffrey, Michael Suman, Phoebe Schramm, and Liuning Zhou. "The 2017 Digital Future Report." *University of Southern California Annenberg.* 2017. http://www.digitalcenter.org/wp-content/uploads/2013/10/2017-Digital-Future-Report.pdf.

Contu, Diane L. "How Resilience Works." *Harvard Business Review.* May 2002. https://hbr.org/2002/05/how-resilience-works.

David, Susan. *Emotional Agility: Get Unstuck, Embrace Change, and Thrive in Work and Life.* New York: Avery an imprint of Penguin Random House, 2016.

Decety, Jean, and Philip Jackson. "The Functional Architecture of Human Empathy." *Behavioral and   Cognitive Neuroscience Reviews* 3, no. 2 (June 2004): 71–100.

"Disruptive Innovation," Clayton Christensen.com. Accessed December 19, 2019, http://claytonchristensen.com/key-concepts/.

Dweck, Carol. *Mindset.* New York: Ballantine Books, 2006.

Ehrenreich, Barbara. *Bright-Sided: How Positive Thinking Is Undermining America.* New York: Henry Holt, 2009.

Emmer, Marc. "95 Percent of New Products Fail. Here Are 6 Steps to Make Sure Yours Don't." *Inc. Magazine*, July 6, 2018. https://www.inc.com/marc -emmer/95-percent-of-new-products-fail-here-are-6-steps-to-make-sure -yours-dont.html.

Equilar. "Equilar | Associated Press CEO Pay Study 2018." May 24, 2018. https://www.equilar.com/reports/57-equilar-associated-press-ceo-pay -study-2018.html.

Feldman, David, and Lee Daniel Kravetz. *Supersurvivors: The Surprising Link Between Suffering and Success.* New York: Harper Collins Publishers, 2014.

Fernandez, Mary. "32 of the BEST Value Propositions (Plus How to Write Your Own)." OptinMonster. Last modified January 7, 2019. https://optin monster.com/32-value-propositions-that-are-impossible-to-resist/.

Fernandez, Rich. "5 Ways to Boost Your Resilience at Work," *Harvard Business Review*. Last modified June 27, 2016. https://hbr.org/2016/06/627 -building-resilience-ic-5-ways-to-build-your-personal-resilience-at-work.

Fottrell, Quentin. "People Spend Most of Their Waking Hours Staring at Screens." *Market Watch*. August 4, 2018. https://www.marketwatch.com /story/people-are-spending-most-of-their-waking-hours-staring-at -screens-2018-08-01.

Fragrantica. "Coca-Cola." Last modified 2019. https://www.fragrantica.com /notes/Coca-Cola-362.html.

Frankl, Viktor Emil. *Man's Search for Meaning: An Introduction to Logotherapy.* New York: Simon & Schuster, 1984.

Fredrickson, Barbara, Michele Tugade, Christian E. Waugh, and Gregory R. Larkin. "What Good Are Positive Emotions in Crises? A Prospective Study of Resilience and Emotions Following the Terrorist Attacks on the United States on September 11, 2001." *Journal of Personality Social Psychology* 84, no. 2 (February 2003): 365–76.

Free Management eBooks. "Emotional Quotient (EQ) and IQ." Accessed July 26, 2018. http://www.free-management-ebooks.com/faqpp/understand ing-03.

Fry, Richard. "Millennials Are the Largest Generation in the U.S. Labor Force." Pew Research Center. April 11, 2018. http://www.pewresearch.org /fact-tank/2018/04/11/millennials-largest-generation-us-labor-force/.

Gallup Strengths Center. "One Assessment to Discover the One True You." Accessed November 1, 2018, https://www.gallupstrengthscenter.com/home /en-us/cliftonstrengths-how-it-works.

Ganchrow, Banji. "Oprah Winfrey's Greatest Accomplishments." Longevity, 2015. https://longevity.media/oprah-winfreys-greatest-accomplishments.

Goldstein, Michael. "Dislocation and Its Discontents: Ride-Sharing's Impact on the Taxi Industry." *Forbes*, June 8, 2018. https://www.forbes.com/sites /michaelgoldstein/2018/06/08/uber-lyft-taxi-drivers/#514e3c8859f0.

Goleman, Daniel, and Richard Boyatzis. "Social Intelligence and the Biology of Leadership." *Harvard Business Review*. September 2008. http://files-au .clickdimensions.com/aisnsweduau-akudz/files/inteligencia-social-y-biolo gia-de-un-lider.pdf.

Graham, Linda. *Bouncing Back: Rewiring Your Brain for Maximum Resilience and Well-Being*. Novato, CA: New World Library, 2013.

Greathouse, John. "7 Lessons from the Beatles' Biggest Failure." *Inc. Magazine*. February 6, 2013. https://www.inc.com/john-greathouse/7-lessons-from -the-beatles-biggest-failure.html.

Guntry, Amy, Patricia Frazier, Howard Tennen, Patricia Tomich, Ty Tashiro, and Crystal Park. "Moderators of the Relation between Perceived and Actual Posttraumatic Growth." *Psychological Trauma: Theory, Research, Practice and Policy* 3 (2011): 61–66.

Healthline. "What Is Diaphragmatic Breathing?" Accessed June 2, 2019. https://www.healthline.com/health/diaphragmatic-breathing.

Healy, Melissa. "For Those in Posh Jobs, Depression May Be Harder to Treat." *Los Angeles Times*, September 21, 2016. https://www.latimes.com /science/sciencenow/la-sci-sn-job-status-depression-20160921-snap-story .html.

Heath, Kathryn, Jill Flynn, Mary Davis Holt, and Diana Faison. *The Influence Effect: A New Path to Power for Women Leaders*. San Francisco: Berrett-Koehler Publishers, 2017.

Help Guide. "Understanding Addiction." Accessed March 23, 2019. https:// www.helpguide.org/harvard/how-addiction-hijacks-the-brain.htm.

Herman, Judith. *Trauma and Recovery: The Aftermath of Violence from Domestic Abuse to Political Terror*. New York: Basic Books, 1992.

Hougaad, Rasmus, Jacqueline Cater, and Gitte Dybkjaer. "Spending 10 Minutes a Day on Mindfulness Subtly Changes the Way You React to Everything." *Harvard Business Review*, January 18, 2017. https://hbr.org/2017/01 /spending-10-minutes-a-day-on-mindfulness-subtly-changes-the-way-you -react-to-everything.

Jackman, Jay, and Myra Strober. "Fear of Feedback." *Harvard Business Review*, April 2003. https://hbr.org/2003/04/fear-of-feedback.

Johnson & Johnson. "Johnson & Johnson Credo." Accessed December 23, 2018. https://www.jnj.com/credo.

Kaplan, Carol P., Sandra Turner, Elaine Norman, and Kathy Stillson. "Promoting Resilience Strategies: A Modified Consultation Model." *Children & Schools* 18, no. 3 (July 1996): 158–68. https://doi.org/10.1093/cs/18.3.158.

Key Step Media. "Emotional and Social Intelligence Competencies: An Overview." Last modified April 11, 2017. https://www.keystepmedia.com /emotional-social-intelligence-leadership-competencies/.

Kim-Cohen, Julia, et al. "Genetic and Environmental Processes in Young Children's Resilience and Vulnerability to Socioeconomic Deprivation." *Child Development* 75, no. 3 (2004): 651–68.

LeanIn.org, and McKinsey & Company. "Women in the Workplace 2016." Last modified September 2016. http://www.mckinsey.com/business-func tions/organization/our-insights/women-in-the-workplace-2016.

Lieberman, Matthew, Naomi Eisenberger, Molly J. Crockett, Sabrina M. Tom, Jennifer H. Pfeifer, and Baldwin M. Way. "Putting Feelings into Words." *Psychological Science* 18, no. 5 (2007): 421–28. https://doi.org /10.1111/j.1467-9280.2007.01916.x.

Lynch, Joe. "'Mad Men' Finale: The Real Story Behind the Coke Jingle That Became a Billboard Hit." *Billboard*, May 28, 2015. https://www.billboard .com/articles/news/6568774/mad-men-finale-buy-the-world-a-coke-song.

Lyon, George Ella. "Where I'm From." George Ella Lyon: Writer & Teacher. Accessed December 23, 2018. http://www.georgeellalyon.com/where.html.

MacMillan, John. "Awards and Achievements." Rockapedia, October 14, 2014. http://www.rockapedia.com/biography/the-beatles/awards-and -achievements.

Masten, Ann, and Dante Cicchetti. "Risk and Resilience in Development and Psychopathology: The Legacy of Norman Garmezy." *Development and Psychopathology* [Special section], 24, 333558, (2012).

Mautz, Scott. "Super-Resilient People Are 6 Times More Likely to Do This 1 Thing, According to New Research." *Inc. Magazine*, May 7, 2019. https:// www.inc.com/scott-mautz/super-resilient-people-are-6-times-more-likely -to-do-this-1-thing-according-to-new-research.html.

McGrath, Rita Gunther, and Philip Dalzell-Payne. "Dancing with Disruption: Incumbents Hit Their Stride." IBM Corporation. Last modified February 2018. https://www.ibm.com/downloads/cas/Y9JBRJ8A.

McKee, Alli. "[Your Company] in 100 Words: How Warby Parker Uses Product to Make Their Story Stick." Medium, November 1, 2017. https:// medium.com/show-and-sell/your-company-in-100-words-e7558b0b1077.

Mehrabian, Albert. *Nonverbal Communication*. Chicago: Aldine-Atherton, 1972.

Miller, Gregory E., and Carsten Wrosch. "You've Gotta Know When to Fold 'Em: Goal Disengagement and Systemic Inflammation in Adolescence." *Psychological Science* 18, no. 9 (September 2007): 773–77. doi:10.1111 /j.1467-9280.2007.01977.x.

Milton Hershey School. "Milton Hershey School FAQs." Accessed June 29, 2019. https://www.mhskids.org/about/faq-2/.

Montminy, Zelana. *21 Days to Resilience: How to Transcend the Daily Grind, Deal with the Tough Stuff, and Discover Your Strongest Self.* New York: Harper Collins, 2016.

Murphy, Mark. "Neuroscience Explains Why You Need to Write Down Your Goals If You Actually Want to Achieve Them." *Forbes,* April 15, 2018. http://www.forbes.com/sites/markmurphy/2018/04/15/neuroscience -explains-why-you-need-to-write-down-your-goals-if-you-actually-want -to-achieve-them/.

National Alliance on Mental Illness. "Mental Health Facts in America." Accessed December 31, 2018. https://www.nami.org/NAMI/media/NAMI -Media/Infographics/GeneralMHFacts.pdf.

National Institute of Mental Health. "Mental Illness." Last modified February 2019. http://www.nimh.nih.gov/health/statistics/prevalence/any-mental -illness-ami-among-adults.shtml.

Pacesetters Unlimited. "Pacesetters Unlimited Online Survey among HBCU Alumni." 2016. www.pacesettersunlimited.org/hbcu.html.

PA Consulting. "Innovation Matters. New Innovation Research." Accessed December 31, 2018. http://www2.paconsulting.com/rs/526-hze-833/images /innovation-matters-report.pdf.

Pak, Eudie. "Walt Disney's Rocky Road to Success." February 21, 2019. https://www.biography.com/news/walt-disney-failures.

Pargament, Kenneth I., Bruce W. Smith, Harold G. Koenig, and Lisa Perez. "Patterns of Positive and Negative Religious Coping with Major Life Stressors." *Journal for the Scientific Study of Religion* 37 (1998): 710–24.

Parmar, Belinda. "The Most Empathetic Companies, 2016." *Harvard Business Review.* Last modified December 20, 2016. https://hbr.org/2016/12/the -most-and-least-empathetic-companies-2016#.

Przybylski, Andrew, and Netta Weinstein. "Can You Connect with Me Now? How the Presence of Mobile Communication Technology Influences Face-to-Face Conversation Quality." *Journal of Social and Personal Relationships Research* 303, no. 3 (2012): 237–46. https://journals.sagepub.com/doi /pdf/10.1177/0265407512453827.

Ranadive, Ameet. "Fixed v. Growth Mindset." March 25, 2016. https:// medium.com/leadership-motivation-and-impact/fixed-v-growth-mindset -902e7d0081b3.

Riess, Helen, and Liz Neporent. *The Empathy Effect: 7 Neurosceience-Based Keys to Transforming the Way We Live, Love, Work and Connect Across Differences.* Boulder: Sounds True, 2018.

Roger, Derek, Nick Petrie, and the Center for Creative Leadership. *Work Without Stress: Building a Resilient Mindset for Lasting Success.* New York: McGraw-Hill Education, 2017.

Rogers, Carl. "Accurate Empathic Understanding." Accessed December 31, 2018. https://www.centerfortheperson.org/pdf/accurate-empathic-under standing.pdf.

Rollins College. "A FAQ Guide to Strengths at Rollins." Accessed November 1, 2018. https://www.rollins.edu/student-affairs/images-docs/faq-guide -strengths.pdf.

Shamay-Tsoory, Simone, Judith Aharon-Peretz, and Danielle Perry. "Two Systems for Empathy: A Double Dissociation Between Emotional and Cognitive Empathy in Inferior Frontal Gyrus Versus Ventromedial Prefrontal Lesions." *Brain: A Journal of Neurology* 132 (Pt 3) (March 2009): 617–27. http://doi.org/10.1093/brain/awn279.

Simpson, Jon, and Forbes Agency Council. "Finding Brand Success in the Digital World." *Forbes*, August 25, 2017. https://www.forbes.com/sites /forbesagencycouncil/2017/08/25/finding-brand-success-in-the-digital -world/#39a16aeb626e.

Singer, Tania, and Claus Lamm. "The Social Neuroscience of Empathy." *Annals of the New York Academy of Sciences* 1156 (March 2009): 85. http://doi .org/10.1111/j.1749-6632.2009.04418.x.

Snow Brains. "Brain Post: How Far Does the Average Human Walk in a Lifetime?" June 20, 2018. https://snowbrains.com/brain-post-how-far-does -the-average-human-walk-in-a-lifetime/.

Srivastava, Lara. "Mobile Phones and the Evolution of Social Behavior." *Behaviour & Information Technology* 24, no. 2 (2005): 111–29. http://doi.org/1 0.1080/01449290512331321910.

Steinberg, Brian. "Study: Young Consumers Switch Media 27 Times an Hour." Ad Age. April 9, 2012. https://adage.com/article/news/study-young -consumers-switch-media-27-times-hour/234008/.

Stibel, Jeff. "Lady Gaga: A Profile in Failure." May 27, 2015. https://www .linkedin.com/pulse/lady-gaga-profile-failure-jeff-stibel/.

———. "Oprah Winfrey: A Profile in Failure." December 5, 2014. https:// www.linkedin.com/pulse/20141205173028-461078-oprah-winfrey-a-pro file-in-failure/.

Strengths Coaching & Training. "StrengthsFinder Domains—4 Areas of Strength." Accessed November 1, 2018. https://strengthscoachingandtrain ing.com/strengthsfinder-clifton-strengths-assessment/strengthsfinder-do mains-categories/.

SWNS. "Americans Check Their Phones 80 Times a Day: Study." *New York Post*, November 8, 2017. https://nypost.com/2017/11/08/americans-check -their-phones-80-times-a-day-study/.

Thompson, Laura Yamhure, C. R. Snyder, Lesa Hoffman, Scott T. Michael, Heather N. Rasmussen, Laura S. Billings, and Danae E. Roberts. "Dispositional Forgiveness of Self, Others and Situations." *Journal of Personality* 73 (2005): 313–59.

Threads Culture. "Core Values Examples." Accessed November 1, 2018. https://www.threadsculture.com/core-values-examples/.

Toussaint, Loren L., David R. Williams, Marc A. Musick, and Susan A. Everson-Rose. "Why Forgiveness May Protect against Depression: Hopelessness as an Explanatory Mechanism." *Personality and Mental Health* 2 (2008): 89–103.

Tugade, Michele M., and Barbara L. Fredrickson. "Resilient Individuals Use Positive Emotions to Bounce Back From Negative Emotional Experiences." *Journal of Personality and Social Psychology* 86, no. 2 (2004): 320–33.

Tugade, Michele, Barbara Fredrickson, and Lisa Feldman Barrett. "Psychological Resilience and Positive Emotional Granularity: Examining the Benefits of Positive Emotions on Coping and Health." *Journal of Personality* 72, no. 6 (December 2004): 1161–90.

Valdesolo, Piercarlo, Jennifer Ouyang, and David DeSteno. "The Rhythm of Joint Action: Synchrony Promotes Cooperative Ability." *Journal of Experimental Social Psychology* 46, no. 4 (July 2010): 693–95. https://www.science direct.com/science/article/pii/S0022103110000430?via%3Dihub.

Van Velsor, Ellen, and Leslie Jean Brittain. "Why Executives Derail: Perspectives across Time and Cultures." *The Academy of Management Executive (1993–2005)* 9, no. 4 (1995): 62–72. http://www.jstor.org/stable/4165289.

Wikipedia. "Blockbuster LLC." Accessed July 1, 2019. https://en.wikipedia .org/wiki/Blockbuster_LLC.

Wikipedia. "Prosody." Accessed December 31, 2018. https://en.wikipedia.org /wiki/Prosody_(linguistics).

Williams, Alina S. "Workplace Stress." Psych Central. Last modified October 8, 2018. https://psychcentral.com/lib/workplace-stress/.

Workplace Options. "Analysis of Global EAP Data Reveals Huge Rise in Depression, Stress, and Anxiety Over Past Three Years." December 16, 2015. https://www.workplaceoptions.com/polls/analysis-of-global-eap-data -reveals-huge-rise-in-depression-stress-and-anxiety-over-past-three-years/.

Wrosch, Carsten, Michael Scheier, Charles Carver, and Richard Schult. "The Importance of Goal Disengagement in Adaptive Self-Regulation: When Giving Up Is Beneficial." *Self and Identity* 2 (2003): 1–20.

Index

181

About the Author

Kristin Harper is CEO of Driven to Succeed, LLC, a leadership development company that provides keynote speaking and brand strategy consulting. An award-winning businesswoman, Kristin has more than thirty years of brand and business experience, from grassroots startups to global iconic brands. She started her first business at the age of fourteen and rose through the ranks to become a global vice president of a Fortune 15 company in her thirties.

Kristin's experience spans both business to consumer and business to business. She built deep general management, brand management, and marketing experience over twenty years at Procter & Gamble, The Hershey Company, and Cardinal Health, respectively. She has led teams to develop strategies, innovation, and equity-building marketing that drive increased sales, profit, and share for global iconic brands, including but not limited to Crest, Oral-B, and Hershey's KISSES. Utilizing proven approaches, Kristin helps businesses, organizations, colleges, and high achieving individuals build clear and compelling brands that drive results.

She is deeply committed to her community as an active lifetime member of Delta Sigma Theta (public service sorority), minister at her church, and cofounder/board president of Pacesetters Unlimited, Inc., which provides mentoring and scholarships to African American youth. Kristin received her bachelor's and MBA degrees from Florida A&M University (FAMU) and understands what it means to lead as a woman. During college, she was elected the first female student government president in nearly a decade and now serves as an appointed member on the FAMU Board of Trustees.

Connect with Kristin at www.KristinHarper.com.